THE UNIVERSE

SCANDINAVIA

The Universe

The splendor, greatness, and beauty of God's creation
How great is our God series

Drejervej 15, DK 2400 Copenhagen NV, Denmark
Email: info@scanpublishing.dk
www.scanpublishing.dk
Author: Austin Sailsbury
Graphic design: Ed Davad
Cover design: Gao Hanyu
Editor: Ben Alex
Coeditor and proof reader: Anne Clark
Consultant: Prof. Johan Fynbo
ISBN: 9788771321135
Printed in China

(Previous page) This false-color image of two density waves in Saturn's A ring was made by the Cassini-Huygens Ultraviolet Imaging Spectrograph instrument. Bright areas indicate the denser regions of the rings. The bright bands in the left part of the image are the 'peaks' of a density wave caused by gravitational stirring of the rings by Saturn's moon, Janus. A smaller density wave in the right half of the image is produced by the moon Pandora. NASA/JPL/SPACE SCIENCE INSTITUTE

How Great Is Our God

THE UNIVERSE

THE SPLENDOR, GREATNESS, AND BEAUTY OF GOD'S CREATION

SCANDINAVIA

Contents

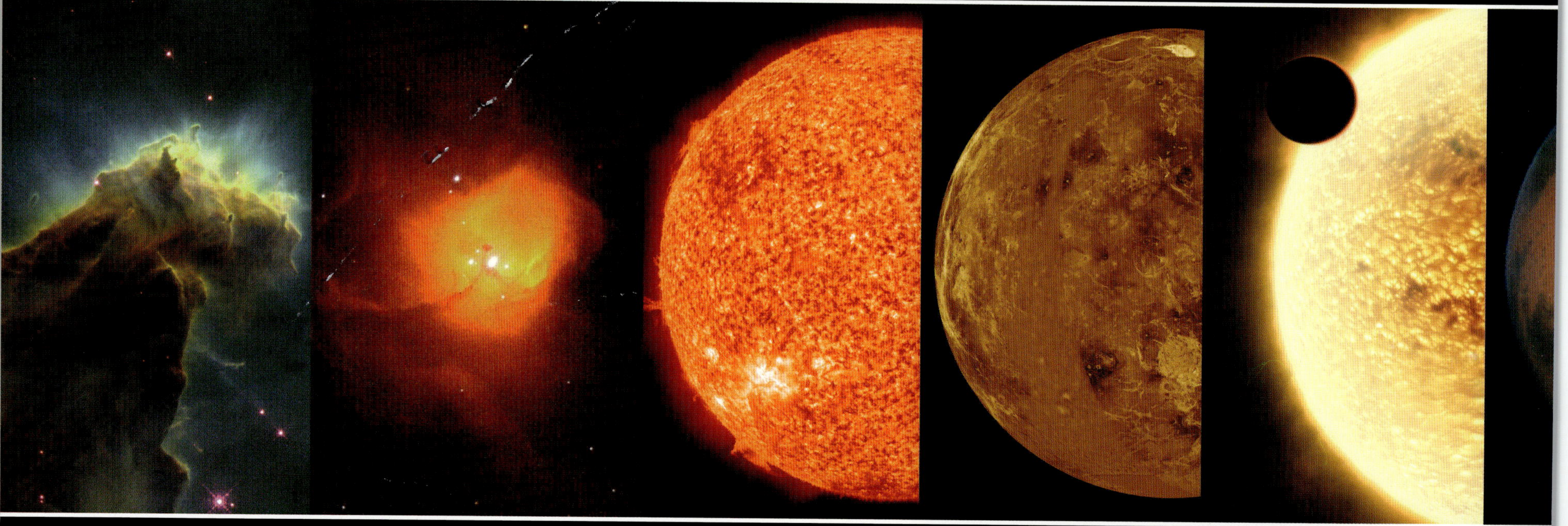

Preface

THIS is a book about the scale, the beauty, and the mystery of the universe. It presupposes not only that the universe is the product of an intelligent designer and has a fixed origin in space and time – it also claims that both of these premises are in agreement with, and not contrary to, modern science. As the British astrophysicist Sir Arthur Eddington said, "The idea of a universal mind or Logos would be, I think, a fairly plausible inference from the present state of scientific theory." As such, this book is ultimately about the scale, beauty, and mystery of the Creator and Sustainer of the universe – the Alpha and Omega, the Almighty God, Creator of atoms and protons, the Initiator of tidal bulges and planetary orbits, the Imagineer of black holes, supernovas, solar flares, and gas giants.

"God's eternal power and character cannot be seen. But from the beginning of creation, God has shown what these are like by all he has made." Romans 1:20 CEV

"I find it quite improbable that such order came out of chaos. There has to be some organizing principle. God to me is a mystery but is the explanation for the miracle of existence, why there is something instead of nothing."

Alan Sandage, American astronomer (1926–2010) and winner of the Crawford prize in astronomy

This eerie, dark structure, resembling an imaginary sea serpent's head, is a column of cool molecular hydrogen gas (two atoms of hydrogen in each molecule) and dust that is an incubator for new stars. The stars are embedded inside finger-like protrusions extending from the top of the nebula. Each "fingertip" is somewhat larger than our own solar system. NASA

Take-off

DURING the past few decades, an incredible view has opened up to us. What the pioneers of science could only glimpse and guess in the past, we now see with our own eyes through powerful telescopes and microscopes.

The deeper we look into nature the more we realize how magnificent and mysterious it is. Every day scientists in all fields find new answers to old questions, or even better, pose new questions to old answers. On and on it goes. Science never arrives because science is built of facts upon which opinions are based, and our perception of facts change constantly with better tools and improved methods. The more we get to know, the more we realize how little we really know. In fact, the most significant discoveries were those that were made while trying to verify erroneous opinions based on misinterpreted facts. As American physicist Robert L. Park put it, "The greatest discoveries of science have always been those that forced us to rethink our beliefs about the universe and our place in it."

As you browse through these pages and look at the facts for yourself, you will clearly see that the universe was made

by God and that He holds it all together in perfect working order. Throughout the centuries, man has looked at the heavens and been drawn to the Creator of it all. This is what God intended - to display who He is in what He has made, to reveal His glory in his handiwork.

Earth is our starting place, and from there we travel out to the surrounding planets in our solar system and then beyond until what we now consider to be very far away is close in comparison to all that lies in the far reaches of space. One can only conclude that the One who holds all this in His hand is truly great.

May you experience wonder and awe from where gratitude and praise naturally flow.

Bon voyage!

"There are two ways to live: you can live as if nothing is a miracle; or you can live as if everything is a miracle."

Albert Einstein, Swiss theoretical physicist (1879–1955)

"Now all we can see of God is like a cloudy picture in a mirror. Later we will see him face to face. We don't know everything, but then we will, just as God completely understands us."

1 Corinthians 13:12 CEV

CHAPTER 1

THE EARTH

"In the beginning God created the heavens and the earth. The earth was barren, with no form of life; it was covered by a roaring ocean and thick darkness. But the Spirit of God was moving over the water." Genesis 1:1 CEV

The Uvs Nuur Basin in Mongolia and the Russian Federation is the northernmost of the enclosed basins of Central Asia. It takes its name from Uvs Nuur Lake, a large, shallow and very saline lake, very important for migrating birds. Inscribed as a UNESCO World Heritage Site in 2003, the site is made up of twelve protected areas representing major biomes of eastern Eurasia. NASA/GSFC/METI/ERSDAC/JAROS, and U.S./Japan ASTER Science Team

Our Home Planet

"When we contemplate the whole globe as one great dewdrop, striped and dotted with continents and islands, flying through space with other stars all singing and shining together as one, the whole universe appears as an infinite storm of beauty."

John Muir, Scottish/American naturalist (1838–1914)

OUR BEAUTIFUL PLANET Earth is unlike any other celestial body we know in the universe. Here, humans, flora, and fauna co-exist within vastly diverse geographic and cultural contexts, and there is no evidence of similar living conditions anywhere else.

But what do we really know about what's out there? We hardly know anything about our own local galaxy, the Milky Way, of which our solar system with its sun and planets are only a tiny part. From earth we can only see about 0.000003% of our local galaxy and only 2,500 of its 200-400 billion stars. When you consider there are hundreds of billions of other galaxies out there beyond the Milky Way – perhaps a hundred times more stars than there are grains of sand on the beaches on Earth – it makes your brain spin. Perhaps it makes you wonder if there could be life on some other distant planet as well.

The odds are favorable. In the Milky Way alone, there are about a hundred billion stars similar to the sun. Two percent of them might have planets like ours. That would make two billion planets in the Milky Way alone with the potential of life in some form.

"The LORD alone is God! He created the heavens and made a world where people can live, instead of creating an empty desert. The LORD alone is God, there are no others."

Isaiah 45:18 CEV

The Earth seen from Apollo 17. NASA

The Great Blue

"When I went to the moon I was a pragmatic test pilot. But when I saw the planet Earth floating in the vastness of space, the presence of divinity became almost palpable, and I knew that life in the universe was not just an accident."

Edgar Mitchell,
Apollo 14 astronaut (1930–)

"This most beautiful system of the sun, planets, and comets, could only proceed from the counsel and dominion of an intelligent and powerful Being."

Isaac Newton,
English physicist (1642–1727)

PLANET EARTH is located about 150 million km (93 miles) from the sun – the perfect position to receive just the right amount of heat and liquid needed to sustain plant and animal life. Along with a unique temperature, some of Earth's other gifts are its abundance of liquid, gaseous, and solid water. The combination of all this, together with a perfect atmospheric balance, makes planet Earth the ideal place for life to thrive. Earth is, without question, a miracle – even in light of our ever-growing scientific understanding of the expanding universe.

Imagine yourself in a spacecraft looking back on Earth from outer space. What you notice at first is the great blue of the oceans that cover more than 70% of the planet's surface. Most of the living things on Earth – both plant and animal – exist within the saltwater of the oceans. Interconnected with local and global climate patterns, wind systems, human food production, oxygen creation, animal migration, and countless other natural systems – it is easy to see why Jacques Cousteau once said, "The sea, once it casts its spell, holds one in its net of wonder forever." Truly, Earth's most impressive geographic attribute – our oceans – are a mysterious universe in themselves.

"With your wisdom and power you created the earth and spread out the heavens. The waters in the heavens roar at your command. You made clouds appear – you send the winds from your storehouse and make lightning flash in the rain."

Jeremiah 10:12-13 CEV

This highly oblique image shot over northwestern part of the African continent captures the curvature of the Earth and shows its atmosphere. You can see clouds and even the occasional thunderhead. From space you can understand how thin and fragile the Earth's atmosphere really is and why we need to protect it. Our atmosphere is composed of 78 percent nitrogen, 21 percent oxygen and 1 percent other constituents, and it shields us from nearly all harmful radiation coming from the Sun and other stars. Earth's atmosphere also protects us from meteors, most of which burn up before they can strike the planet. Affected by changes in solar activity, the upper atmosphere contributes to weather and climate on Earth.
NASA/JPL/UCSD/JSC

The Heart of the Earth

OUR HOME PLANET was born a long time ago in the heart of the solar system. Deep down under the blue oceans, some 5000 km (3,107 miles) under the Earth's crust, is a core of hot iron believed to be roughly the same temperature as that of the surface of the Sun (5,500 degrees Celsius). This core causes the upper layers of Earth's geology to be extremely active – continuously moving the broken tectonic plates of the outer crust on which landmasses float around like lost rafts. Therefore, the continents are extremely vulnerable to earthquakes and other natural disasters.

The diameter of the Earth is 12,756 km (7,926 miles), and it weighs 5,973,700,000,000,000,000,000 tons. It rotates upon its axis every 23 hours 56 minutes with a speed of nearly 1000 km/h (621 miles/hour), and it takes 365 days 6 hours for it to orbit the Sun, traveling roughly 100,000 km/h (62,137 miles/hour). Still you can sit quietly on a beach and look into space or watch from a space ship, and the Earth doesn't seem to be moving at all. It just sits there dressed in white clouds and covered with blue oceans and green-brown lands like a precious jewel against the black backdrop of space with its faraway planets.

"This is what the LORD says: 'Heaven is my throne, the earth is my footstool. What kind of house could you build for me? In what place will I rest?'"

Isaiah 66:1 CEV

"Living on Earth may be expensive, but it includes an annual free trip around the Sun."

Anonymous

"There are no passengers on Spaceship Earth. We are all crew."

Marshall McLuhan, Canadian communication theorist (1911–1980)

Arching fountain of a Pahoehoe approximately 10 m high issuing from the western end of the 0740 vents, a series of spatter cones 170 m long, south of Pu'u Kahaualea. WIKIMEDIA COMMONS

The Breath of Life

"We are like tenant farmers chopping down the fence around our house for fuel when we should be using nature's inexhaustible sources of energy – sun, wind, and tide. ... I'd put my money on the sun and solar energy. What a source of power! I hope we don't have to wait until oil and coal run out before we tackle that."

Thomas Edison,
American inventor
(1847–1931)

THE ATMOSPHERE is a layer of gas above the Earth's surface. It forms a barrier between Earth and outer space that protects us from dangerous solar radiation. Like a comfortable blanket around the Earth, it reduces temperature extremes between day and night so the average temperature of the surface of the Earth is 15 degrees Celsius (59 degrees F).

Our atmosphere is divided into different layers according to temperature and composition. Human life occurs in the troposphere, which extends to about 10 km (6 miles) above the Earth's surface and determines weather on Earth. The troposphere gives way to the stratosphere, mesosphere, thermosphere, and, at about 500 km (310 miles) above Earth's surface, the exosphere. The higher you go, the thinner the atmosphere gets until at about 100 km (62 miles) above the Earth it extends into space where there is no air or heat.

The protective ozone layer in the lower part of the stratosphere (20-30 km/6 mi above the Earth) is important for life on Earth. Like a huge shield around the planet, it absorbs 98 percent of the harmful ultraviolet light (UV) from the sun that would otherwise break down our DNA molecules and eventually kill all life. The ozone layer is vulnerable to human activity, such as the use of aerosol sprays and chemicals used in refrigeration and industrial cleaning. Such compounds break down the ozone molecules and make them unable to absorb Sun's ultraviolet radiation. Consequently, unabsorbed and dangerous ultraviolet-B radiation is able to reach the Earth's surface especially through the ozone holes above the north and south poles.

If you were looking from a space ship, you would notice a blue rim around the Earth. This is the lower layer of the atmosphere. It appears like this because blue light is scattered by the gasses in the atmosphere more than other wavelengths, giving the Earth a hazy blue halo. The blue of the oceans is a reflection of the great blue of the sky.

"You alone are the LORD. You made the heavens, even the highest heavens, and all their starry host, the earth and all that is on it, the seas and all that is in them. You give life to everything, and the multitudes of heaven worship you."

Nehemiah 9:6 NIV

Intelligent Design

THE ATMOSPHERE is held in place by Earth's gravitational force, which pulls everything towards its center. The gravitational pull on an object is measured as weight. So if you weigh a hundred kilos, don't worry too much about it. Your weight only reveals how strong the Earth's pull is on you. You may want to be more worried about mass, which is different from weight. Mass is related to how much there is of an object.

Objects that take up space and have mass are called matter. Everything that has existence is made up of matter – from the smallest grain of sand to the biggest galaxy. Matter is simply a gathering of atoms, atomic nucleuses with electrons whirling around them. Every element has a different nucleus and a different arrangement of electrons. The table in front of you is different from the window pane because they are made up of different atoms and electrons. The table looks solid and yet it is mostly empty space – just like the universe is almost entirely empty space. In fact, every atom is 99.9999999999999 percent empty space, which means that all the matter that makes up Earth's seven billion people could be in a very small place. If you could squeeze all the empty space out of all the atoms of the entire human race they could fit within a sugar cube! Or if you can imagine yourself as one single nucleus somewhere in London, your electrons would be orbiting around you through Lyon, Hamburg, Copenhagen, and so on. The space between would be empty.

But what's really amazing is that all the atoms that make up the universe are interconnected through a consciousness which is a mystery to science. No two atoms can be the same, so if you changed the orbit of the electrons in an atom in your hand – for instance by rubbing your hands and thereby changing their temperature – every surrounding atom would respond by alternating their orbits. So the littlest change of an atom in your hand affects the whole universe. As the British theoretical physicist Paul Dirac once said, "Pick a flower on Earth and you move the farthest star." There is certainly meaning and structure in the universe from the smallest atom to the biggest galaxy! Some scientists call it intelligent design.

"The statistical probability that organic structures and the most precisely harmonized reactions that typify living organisms would be generated by accident is zero."

Ilya Prigogine, Belgian chemist, recipient of two Nobel Prizes (1917–2003)

"You have always been God – long before the birth of the mountains, even before you created the earth and the world."

Psalm 90:2 CEV

This artist's conception symbolically represents complex organic molecules, known as polycyclic aromatic hydrocarbons, seen in the early universe. These large molecules, comprised of carbon and hydrogen, are considered among the building blocks of life. Polycyclic aromatic hydrocarbons are pervasive in galaxies like our own Milky Way, and play a significant role in star and planet formation. NASA/JPL-Caltech

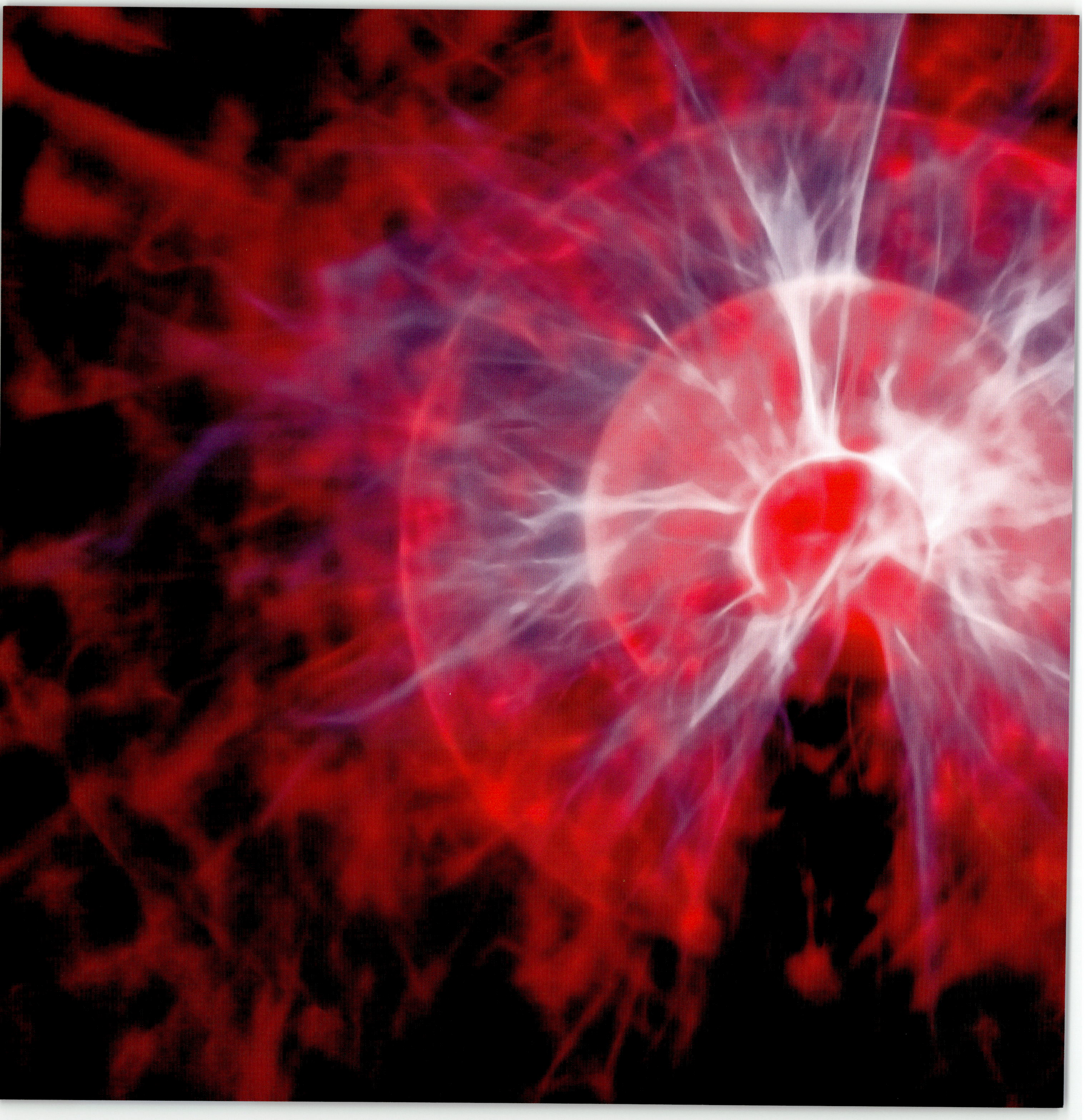

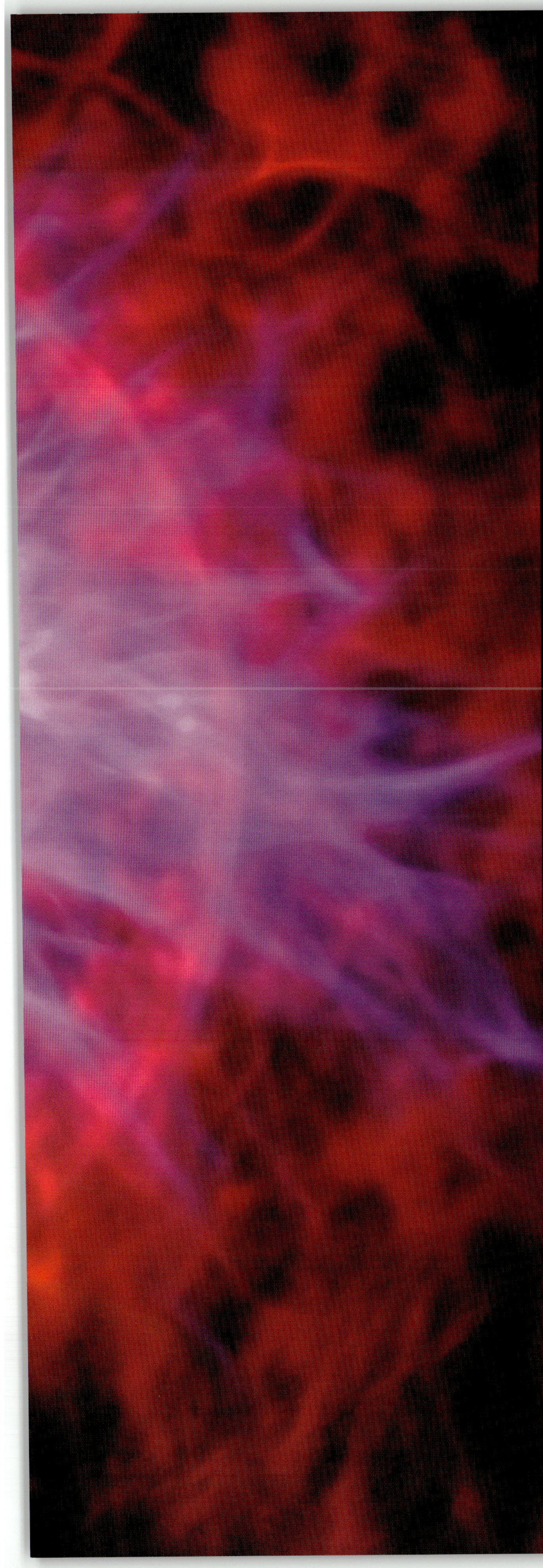

The God Particle

ATOMS ARE CREATION'S building blocks. Scientists have known that for centuries. Already in the 4th century BC a Greek philosopher, Democritus, developed the idea of atoms by breaking a piece of matter in half and then breaking it in half again, over and over again. He asked, How many breaks will it take until the piece of matter can be broken no further? Democritus thought it ended at some point. This basic piece of matter he called an atom, the smallest unit of an element. Today we know that an atom is much smaller than Democritus could imagine. Although we cannot see atoms even in a microscope, we know they are there with their neutrons, protons, and electrons.

But what has puzzled scientists up to this very day is this: How was mass first formed? How did it happen that something came out of nothing? Fifty years ago a British scientist named Peter Higgs developed a theory concerning an unknown particle he thought might have given substance to everything in the universe. The "Higgs boson" (a field carrying particles) could have enabled the energy of some creational force to arrange atoms into mass. It could also be the particle that holds the physical fabric of the Universe together.

In July of 2012, this theory was verified with a certainty of 99%. The discovery of Higgs boson in the large Hadron Collider at CERN in Switzerland was one of the greatest achievements in modern science. The discovery of this unknown particle field is the closest we can come to the moment of creation.

"He alone stretches out the heavens and treads on the waves of the sea."

Job 9:8 NIV

"There is no matter as such. All matter originates and exists only by virtue of a force which brings the particle of an atom to vibration and holds this most minute solar system of the atom together. We must assume behind this force the existence of a conscious and intelligent mind. This mind is the matrix of all matter."

Max Planck, German theoretical physicist, founder of the quantum theory (1858–1947)

Okay To Go

"Why did they send a scientist? They should have sent a poet!"

Ellie Arroway (Jodie Foster) in the movie *Contact* (1997)

"It is a wholesome and necessary thing for us to turn again to the earth and in the contemplation of her beauties to know of wonder and humility."

Rachel Carson, American marine biologist (1907–1964)

AS WE CONTINUE our journey through the atmosphere and further into space, an immense and beautiful scenery opens up before our eyes. Just ahead is the Milky Way, our own galaxy with its more than 200 billion stars. Ours is a relatively small galaxy, almost one million trillion kilometers across. And yet it takes 100,000 years for light to cross it at its speed of almost 300,000 km (186,411 miles) per second.

The Milky Way is just an average spiral galaxy among the billions of other galaxies that make up the visible universe. In one of its spiral arms, tucked away in a relatively quiet neighborhood, is our sun and its planets. At the moment, we can observe 30,000 million million million (18 zeroes) stars just like our own sun, some bigger some smaller. And we know of roughly 350 billion large galaxies and 7,000 billion smaller dwarf galaxies further out in space. What's beyond the limits of our sight we don't yet know – perhaps trillions and trillions more galaxies. Who knows, these trillions of galaxies could be the atomic structure of an even larger entity!

But for now, let's make small moves and hop from planet to planet in our own solar system. So far we haven't been able to personally visit any planet other than our closest neighbor, the moon. But we did land Curiosity, an exploratory, unmanned vehicle, on Mars in July of 2012.

First stop is the moon. Before we go on, it might be helpful to look back on our blue home planet Earth and establish the right perspective for further exploration. Seen from space, the Earth is the brightest and most beautiful of the nine planets that orbit around the sun. Astronaut Neil Armstrong put it well after the Apollo 11 moon landing in 1969 when he said, "It suddenly struck me that the tiny pea, pretty and blue, was the Earth. I put up my thumb and shut one eye, and my thumb blotted out the planet Earth. I didn't feel like a giant. I felt very, very small."

*"Our Lord and Ruler, your name is wonderful everywhere on earth!
You let your glory be seen in the heavens above.
With praises from children
and from tiny infants, you have built a fortress.
It makes your enemies silent,
and all who turn against you are left speechless."*

Psalm 8:1-2 CEV

Located in the Large Magellanic Cloud, the Tarantula Nebula is one of the largest star-forming regions close to the Milky Way. NASA/JPL/Caltech

"When I send clouds over the earth, and a rainbow appears in the sky, I will remember my promise to you and to all other living creatures. Never again will I let floodwaters destroy all life."

Genesis 9:14-15 CEV

Image based largely on observations from the Moderate Resolution Imaging Spectroradiometer (MODIS) on July 11, 2005. Small gaps in MODIS' coverage between overpasses, as well as Antarctica, have been filled in using GOES weather satellites and the latest version of the NASA Blue Marble. NASA

CHAPTER 2

THE MOON

"He made the moon to mark the seasons; the sun knows its time for setting. O Lord, how manifold are your works! In wisdom have you made them all."

Psalm 104:19,24 ESV

Our Constant Companion

SINCE 1969 when Neil Armstrong first placed his feet on the moon's dusty surface and said, "That's one small step for man, one giant leap for mankind," eleven other American astronauts have paid our cosmic companion a visit and brought back almost 400 kilos of rock from that rocky and inhospitable place. The moon is covered with craters, mountains, basins, maria, and inactive volcanoes. This material has been used to develop a geological understanding of the moon's origins. The moon has no atmosphere and only traces of ice in permanently shadowed craters at its poles. It is believed that the moon has an iron core beneath its cratered surface and multi-leveled mantles.

Among the over 130 moons in our solar system, the moon is the Earth's only natural satellite. Throughout the ages, the moon has been a nightly reminder that there are things in creation beyond our grasp – visible but untouchable, ever changing but faithfully in its course. The full moon has also been the reason for many spooky beliefs that have shrouded the moon in fear and superstition. Many of these beliefs have survived to this very day and may be dismissed with future missions to the moon by government funded, as well as privately funded, efforts. The moon remains, due to the Outer Space Treaty, free to all nations to explore for peaceful purposes.

"God stores water in clouds, but they don't burst, and he wraps them around the face of the moon."

Job 26:8-9 CEV

"He lets the moon and the stars rule each night. God's love never fails."

Psalm 136:9 CEV

"What was most significant about the lunar voyage was not that men set foot on the moon but that they set eye on the earth."

Norman Cousins, American professor and world peace activist (1915–1990)

One of a series of photos of the moon and Earth's atmosphere as seen from the International Space Station over a period of time that covered a number of orbits by the orbital outpost. NASA

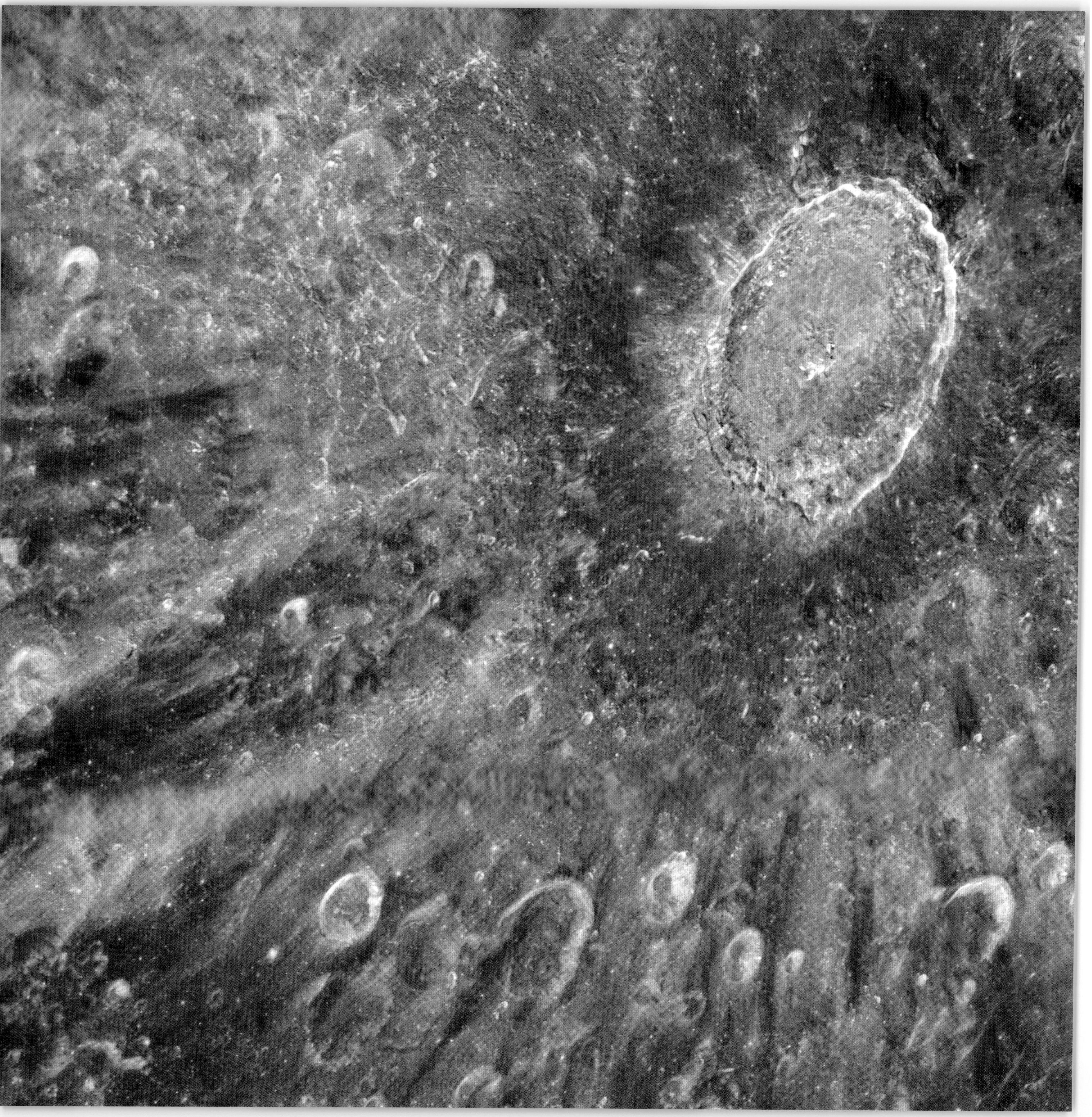

Two Faces of the Moon

ALTHOUGH THE MOON fully orbits the Earth every 29.5 days, only one of its faces, the Man in the Moon, is visible in the night sky. The reason for the moon's inability to "spin" fully as it orbits the Earth is gravity. Due to the close proximity between the Earth and moon, there is an immense gravitational interplay between the two causing what is called synchronous rotation in the moon. Synchronous rotation means that the moon rotates on its axis in roughly the same amount of time that it rotates around the Earth – with the same face always turned toward Earth. This is why only one half of the moon, the "near" side, is ever visible from Earth and why the "far" or "back" side of the moon never comes into full view.

It wasn't until the age of 20th-century space exploration that it was possible to study the "back" side of the moon. Though for millennia the moon had been the subject of great curiosity and imaginative speculation, we now know what the moon's mysterious "back" side looks like – heavily cratered and without the many lunar seas that are so recognizable on the moon's near side.

An eternal satellite with two distinct faces: one, a trusted symbol of the march of time and seasons and the other, a shrouded world just beyond our view.

"We will build new ships to carry man forward into the universe, to gain a new foothold on the moon and to prepare for new journeys to the worlds beyond our own."

George W. Bush,
former U.S. President (1946–)

*"You created the moon to tell us the seasons.
The sun knows when to set, and you made the darkness, so the animals in the forest could come out at night."*

Psalm 104:19-20 CEV

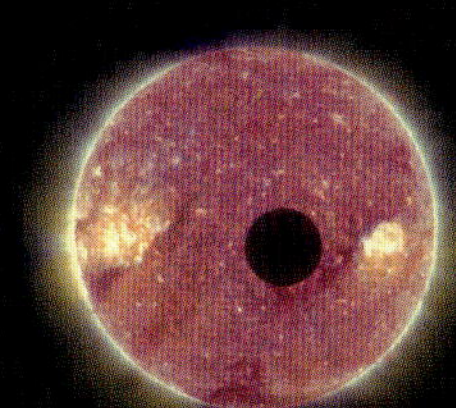

This transit of the moon across the sun on Feb. 25, 2007, could not be seen from Earth. NASA

This mottled landscape showing the impact crater Tycho is among the most violent-looking places on our Moon. NASA, ESA, D. EHRENREICH (INSTITUT DE PLANÉTOLOGIE ET D'ASTROPHYSIQUE DE GRENOBLE (IPAG)/CNRS/ UNIVERSITÉ JOSEPH FOURIER)

The Light of The Moon

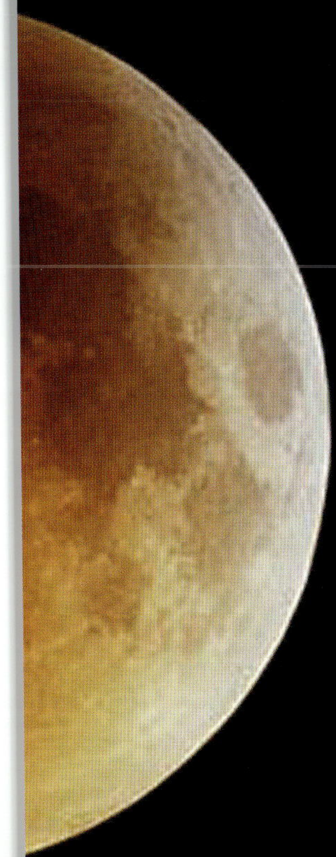

FROM OUR PERSPECTIVE on Earth, the moon seems to be roughly the same size as the sun and be a similar source of light in the sky. And yet, despite the familiar blue glow of moonlight, the moon makes no light of its own. It merely reflects light from the sun back towards the Earth. As it cycles through its waxing and waning phases, the moon itself never physically changes, but the amount of light reflected (and, therefore, the moon's appearance) varies depending on the orbital patterns of sun, Earth, and moon.

Since the moon has no atmosphere to hold light, the universe around it looks totally black. But to us humans on Earth, "moonlight" is our reminder that though the sun may be out of view during the night, its light is still shining powerfully throughout the solar system, so powerfully, in fact, that even when it is completely hidden from view, it is making other things visible.

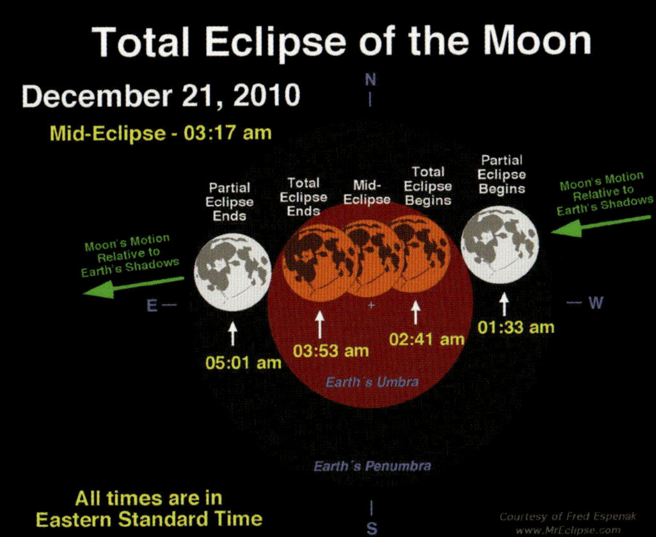

"Jesus told us that God is light and doesn't have any darkness in him. Now we are telling you. If we say that we share in life with God and keep on living in the dark, we are lying and are not living by the truth. But if we live in the light, as God does, we share in life with each other."

1 John 1:5-7a CEV

"Moonlight drowns out all but the brightest stars."

J.R.R. Tolkien,
British author (1892–1973),
The Lord of the Rings

Path of the moon through Earth's umbral and penumbral shadows during the Total Lunar Eclipse of December 21, 2010. FRED ESPENAK/NASA'S GODDARD SPACE FLIGHT CENTER

"Love builds up the broken wall and straightens the crooked path. Love keeps the stars in the firmament and imposes rhythm on the ocean tides. Each of us is created of it and, I suspect, each of us was created for it." Maya Angelou, American author and poet (1928–)

The Moon and the Ocean Tides

SINCE THE DAWN of their creation, the moon and the Earth have been locked in an intimate dance – a waltz of turning and spinning, waxing and waning, gravity and motion. For ages, this dance has played out in the night sky with the history of humanity as its audience and the waters of the seas its timekeeper.

It is commonly known that the moon has a great effect on the Earth's ocean tides. But the reason why and how the moon affects the rise and fall of Earth's great waters is, not surprisingly, the result of gravitational forces. Although the gravitational pull of the sun is nearly 200 times stronger than that of the moon, the tidal force from the moon on the Earth and its oceans are about twice as strong as those of the sun. Though the moon's gravity pulls on all the parts of Earth, it is most easily observed in the changing ocean tides (or tidal bulges). In the tides we can observe how the moon's gravity is always pulling the oceans towards itself thus causing higher tides for oceans facing the moon and lower tides for oceans facing away (on the opposite side of Earth).

"You rule the day and the night, and you put the moon and the sun in place. You made the summer and winter and gave them to the earth."

Psalm 74:16-17 CEV

This image was constructed by overlaying the Hubble Advanced Camera for Surveys image of the Apollo 17 landing region within the Taurus-Littrow valley, taken on Dec. 16, 2005, with a digital-terrain model acquired by the Apollo program to provide a perspective view looking from west to east up the valley. NASA, ESA, and J. Garvin (NASA/GSFC)

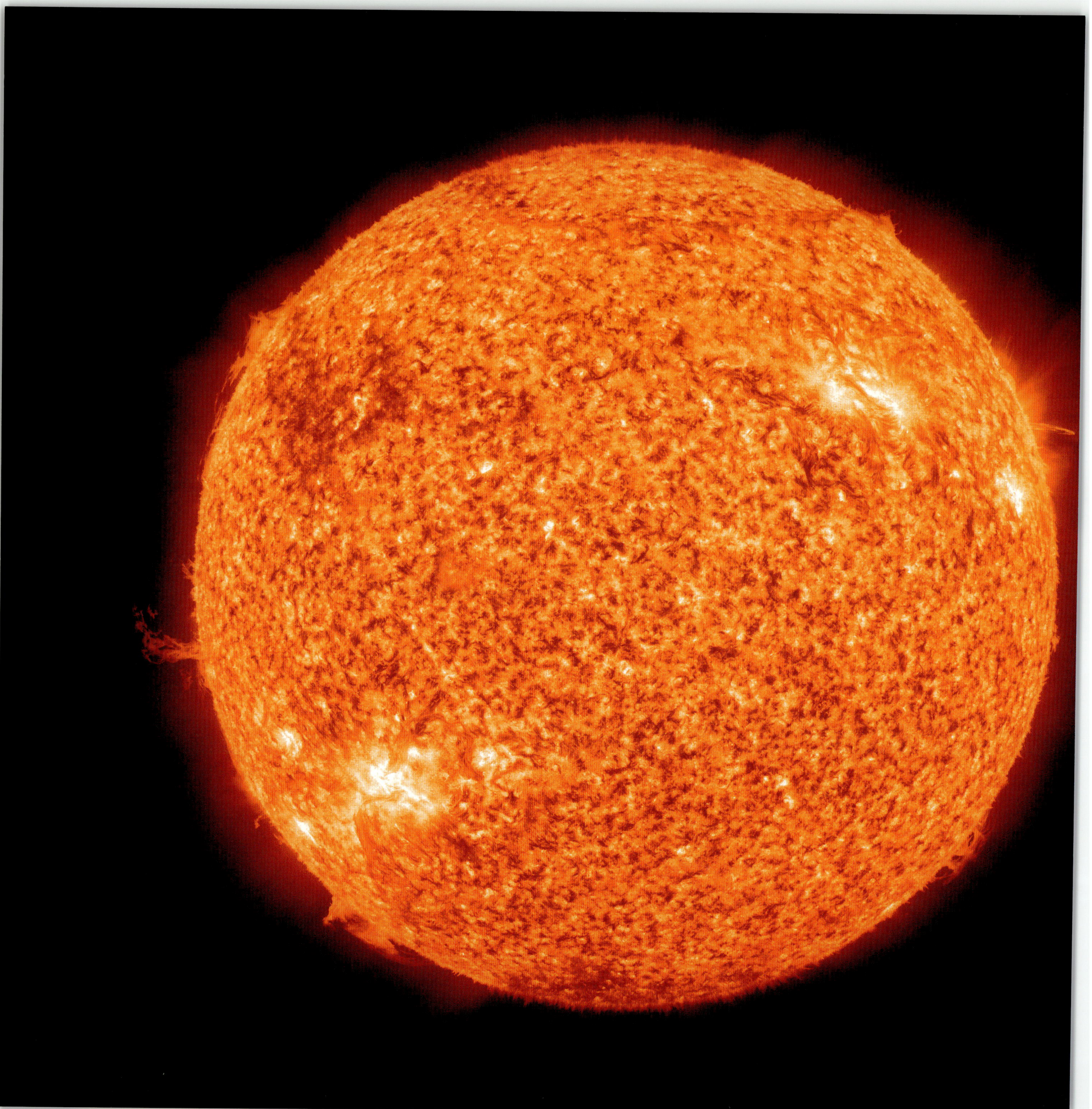

CHAPTER 3
THE SUN

"At the age of 9, I found out that the stars are glowing balls of gas. I also found out that the sun is a star but really close and that the stars are all suns except really far away. I didn't know any physics or mathematics at that time, but I could imagine how far you'd have to move the sun away from us till it was only as bright as a star. It was in that library, reading that book, that the scale of the universe opened up to me. There was something beautiful about it."

Carl Sagan, American astronomer and cosmologist (1934–1996)

"God said, 'I command light to shine!' And light started shining. God looked at the light and saw that it was good. He separated light from darkness and named the light 'Day' and the darkness 'Night.'"

Genesis 1:3-4 CEV

The Sun photographed by the Atmospheric Imaging Assembly (AIA 304) of NASA's Solar Dynamics Observatory. NASA

The Heart of The Milky Way

THE SUN IS THE STAR at the center of the solar system that includes Earth and its eight neighboring planets and their satellites. Its average distance from Earth is almost 150 million km (93,205,678 miles). Classified as a yellow dwarf star, the sun is far from the largest type of stars in the universe. It is a medium-sized star with a diameter of 1.4 million km (869,919 miles) and a mass 333,000 times more than the Earth. It takes the sun 609 hours and 7 minutes to rotate once fully. That is over 25 earth days.

Astronomers believe that the sun has about five billion years worth of its hydrogen fuel left to burn before it dies and turns into a "red giant" and then, ultimately, a "white dwarf" star. In the meantime, the sun is a fiery and dependable source of light and heat – producing 400 trillion watts of energy every second and losing 4.5 million tons of mass per second.

"Someday, after mastering the winds, the waves, the tides and gravity, we shall harness for God the energies of love, and then, for a second time in the history of the world, man will have discovered fire."

Teilhard de Chardin,
French paleontologist
and Jesuit priest (1881–1955)

"The Scriptures say, 'God commanded light to shine in the dark.' Now God is shining in our hearts to let you know that his glory is seen in Jesus Christ."

2 Corinthians 4:6 CEV

30 Doradus is the brightest star-forming region in our galactic neighbourhood and home to the most massive stars ever seen. The nebula resides 170 000 light-years away in the Large Magellanic Cloud, a small, satellite galaxy of our Milky Way. No known star-forming region in our galaxy is as large or as prolific as 30 Doradus. NASA

The Heat of the Sun

LIKE MOST STARS, the sun is primarily made of burning hydrogen gas. At its super hot core (where temperatures are estimated to be 15 million degrees Celsius), hydrogen is "burned" to create helium during the process of nuclear fusion. Scientists believe that at its core the sun is converting 600 million metric tons of hydrogen to helium every single second. Another estimate claims that each second during this powerful process, the sun's core produces the same amount of energy as ten billion hydrogen bombs. As the energy from this nuclear process moves out in waves from the sun's core to its surface (or photosphere), it cools and becomes the light and heat that warms the Earth.

At the sun's incomprehensibly hot center, a chemical reaction – the fusion of hydrogen into helium – repeated ad infinitum every second of every day since the dawn of time is the source of the energy that allows life to exist on Earth. It is no wonder that the ancients worshipped the sun and its power. Seen from Earth as a small yellowish ball traveling daily from east to west, the sun is really an unfathomable source of power: a great light in the dark expanse of the universe.

"In the heavens a tent is set up for the sun. It rises like a bridegroom and gets ready like a hero eager to run a race. It travels all the way across the sky. Nothing hides from its heat."

Psalm 19:4-6 CEV

"The sun, with all the planets revolving around it and depending on it, can still ripen a bunch of grapes as though it had nothing else in the universe to do." Galileo Galilei, Italian astronomer (1564–1642)

An artist's impression of the extrasolar planet HD 189733b seen here with its parent star looming behind. The planet is slightly larger than our own Solar System's Jupiter. Its atmosphere is a scorching eight hundred degrees Celsius. Astronomers have found that the sunset on HD 189733b would look similar to a hazy red sunset on Earth.

"When I admire the wonders of a sunset or the beauty of the moon, my soul expands in the worship of the creator."

Mahatma Gandhi,
Indian peace activist
(1869–1948)

"I often think of the heavens your hands have made, and of the moon and stars you put in place. Then I ask, 'Why do you care about us humans? Why are you concerned for us weaklings?' You made us a little lower than you yourself, and you have crowned us with glory and honor."

Psalm 8:3-5 CEV

One of the top candidates for the title of "Milky Way stellar heavyweight champion" was, until now, Pismis 24-1, a bright young star that lies in the core of the small open star cluster Pismis 24 (the bright stars in the image) about 8,000 light-years away from Earth. NASA, ESA AND JESÚS MAÍZ APELLÁNIZ (INSTITUTO DE ASTROFÍSICA DE ANDALUCÍA, SPAIN). ACKNOWLEDGEMENT: DAVIDE DE MARTIN (ESA/HUBBLE)

The Sun IS the Solar System

THE SUN IS SO MASSIVE it makes up more than 99% of the mass of the solar system. Some astronomers estimate that the sun actually constitutes 99.8% of the mass with Jupiter making up most of the remaining 0.2%. Earth represents only a small fraction of that 0.2%.

To get an idea of proportions, if the sun were hollow, it could contain one million earths inside of it. Thinking of the sun in this way throws a stark light on the reality of scale in our solar system and our galaxy. We humans and our endeavors are but miniscule details in a seemingly limitless creation. How often do we overestimate our own importance? How often do we underappreciate the greatness of the God who made it all?

Even more, consider that a million earths inside a hypothetical "hollow sun" is nothing compared to the billions of stars (many of them much greater than the sun) in the countless galaxies yet to be discovered.

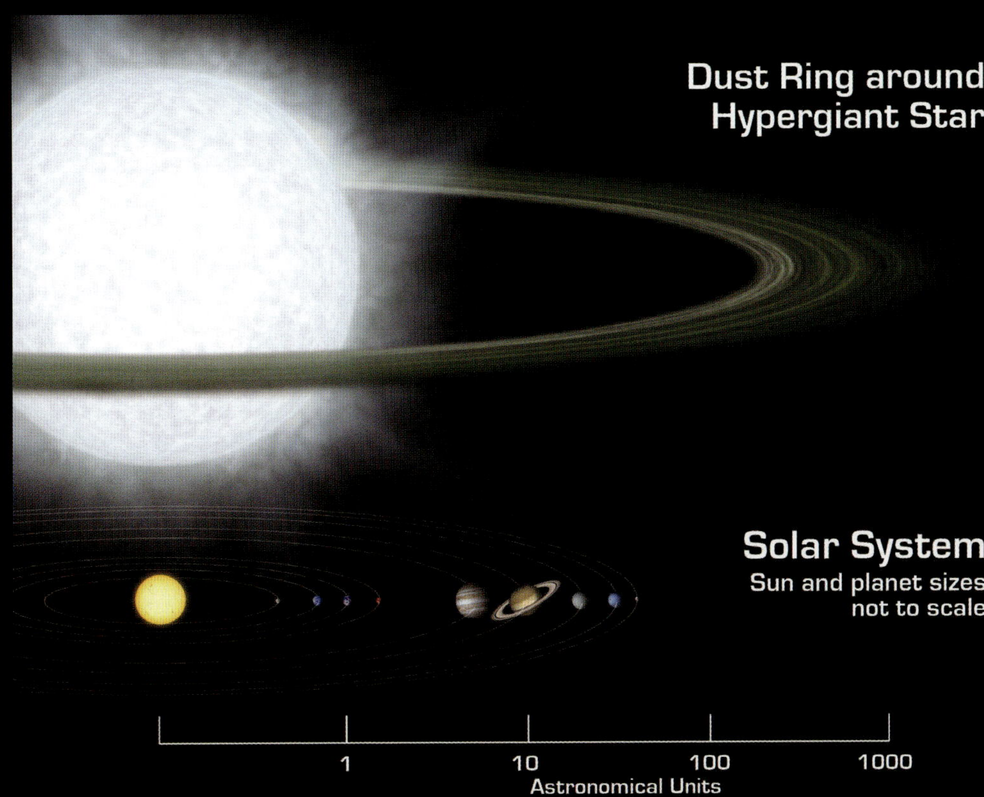

This illustration compares the size of a gargantuan star and its surrounding dusty disk (top) to that of our solar system. Astronomers believe these disks might contain the early "seeds" of planets, or possibly leftover debris from planets that already formed. The stars are about 100 times wider than the sun, or big enough to encompass an orbit equivalent to Earth's.Hypergiant stars are the puffed-up, aging descendants of the most massive class of stars, called "O" stars. The stars are so massive that their cores ultimately collapse under their own weight, triggering incredible explosions called supernovae. If any planets circled near the stars during one of these blasts, they would most likely be destroyed. NASA/JPL-CALTECH

"Men love to wonder, and that is the seed of science."

Ralph Waldo Emerson,
American poet and essayist (1803–1882)

The Light of the Sun

THE SUN IS EARTH'S brightest ally in growing and sustaining life. It is the sun's powerful light which throws the rest of our solar system into visibility allowing astronomers, satellites, and telescopes to study stellar bodies.

It takes light 5.5 hours to travel from the sun to Pluto but only 8.3 minutes to reach Earth. Light from the next nearest star, Proxima Centauri, takes 4.2 years to arrive here at Earth. Without the sun's light, life on Earth would be dramatically different (if it could exist at all). Unfortunately, over time and in permanent darkness, no one would be able to see what it was like.

"Nothing on earth is more beautiful than the morning sun."

Ecclesiastes 11:7 CEV

"I believe in Christianity as I believe that the sun has risen: not only because I see it, but because by it I see everything else."

C. S. Lewis,
British author and professor of literature (1898–1963)

The star-forming region NGC 3603 contains one of the most impressive massive young star clusters in the Milky Way. Bathed in gas and dust, the cluster formed in a huge rush of star formation thought to have occurred around a million years ago. NASA, ESA AND THE HUBBLE HERITAGE (STSCI/AURA)-ESA/HUBBLE COLLABORATION

"If you want to be reminded of the love of the Lord, just watch the sunrise."

Jeannette Walls,
American author (1960–),
Half Broke Horses

"People come, and people go, but still the world never changes. The sun comes up, the sun goes down; it hurries right back to where it started from. The wind blows south, the wind blows north; round and round it blows, over and over again."

Ecclesiastes 1:4-6 CEV

On August 27, 2011, International Space Station astronaut Ron Garan used a high-definition camera to film one of the 16 sunrises astronauts see each day. This image shows the rising sun as the station flew along a path between Rio de Janeiro, Brazil, and Buenos Aires, Argentina. NASA

The Sun's Influence

JUST AS THE LIGHT of the sun travels great distances from its surface out into space, so too does the sun's magnetic power captivate, quite literally, the planets of our solar system. Thought to be the result of the rotational behavior of the Sun's electrically charged gases, the heliosphere – the sun's immensely powerful magnetic field – reaches out to the limits of our solar system and holds it together. In this way the sun provides another display of its unequaled influence on the Earth and its neighbors. Not only are we dependent on the sun's daily offering of light and heat to sustain life as we know it, but it seems we too need the sun's strong pull to keep us from floating into the dark infinite of space.

"If we can see the tails of comets fly off in the direction opposed to the sun with an accelerated velocity, and if we believe these tails to be matter and not optical illusions or mere tracks of vibrating disturbance, then we must admit a force in that direction, and we may establish that it is caused by the sun if it always depends upon his position and distance."

James Clerk Maxwell, Scottish physicist (1831–1879)

"Although your people live in darkness, they will see a bright light. Although they live in the shadow of death, a light will shine on them."

Matthew 4:16 CEV

"The center of the earth is not the center of the universe, but only of gravity and of the lunar sphere. All the spheres revolve about the sun as their mid-point, and therefore the sun is the center of the universe."

Nicolaus Copernicus, Polish astronomer (1473–1543)

Astronomers have obtained the first clear look at a dusty disk closely encircling a massive baby star, providing direct evidence that massive stars do form in the same way as their smaller brethren—and closing an enduring debate. This artist's concept shows what such a massive disk might look like.

ESO/L. CALÇADA

The Life and Death of the Sun

A STAR'S COMPOSITION and mass will determine the length of its life – how long its light burns in the blackness of space. Although enormous compared to the Earth, the sun has a small mass compared to other known stars. For example, the star known as Betelgeuse has an estimated diameter of 750 times that of the sun. The more massive a star, the more spectacular its brightness, and the more impressive its death will be.

Known as a "main sequence" star, the sun is in the prime of its life cycle because it is still burning through the hydrogen fuel of its core. When those gasses eventually run out – astronomers estimate approximately five billion years – the sun will no longer produce such powerful light and energy and will no longer be able to counterbalance the forces of gravity acting upon it. The sun will lose mass and collapse as it transitions from a red giant star into a yellow dwarf star and eventually into a white dwarf star – reduced from its current size to approximately the same size as the Earth, less than one percent of its current diameter. At this phase in the life of the sun, it will no longer be producing energy through nuclear fusion, but it will still be extremely hot – a glowing ember at the end of a spectacular life.

"He puts mighty kings to shame, and takes away their power. God turns darkness to light; he makes nations strong, then shatters their strength."

Job 12:21-23 CEV

"A star is drawing on some vast reservoir of energy by means unknown to us. This reservoir can scarcely be other than the subatomic energy which, it is known exists abundantly in all matter; we sometimes dream that man will one day learn how to release it and use it for his service. The store is well nigh inexhaustible, if only it could be tapped. There is sufficient in the Sun to maintain its output of heat for 15 billion years."

Sir Arthur Stanley Eddington,
British astrophysicist
(1882–1944)

This artist's concept depicts a type of dead star called a pulsar and the surrounding disk of rubble. The pulsar was once a massive star until about 100,000 years ago when it blew up in a supernova explosion and scattered dusty debris into space. Some of that debris was captured into what astronomers refer to as a "fallback disk," now circling the remaining stellar core, or pulsar. The disk resembles protoplanetary disks around young stars, out of which planets are thought to be born. NASA/JPL-CALTECH

Solar Flares

"I have satisfied myself that the [cosmic] rays are not generated by the formation of new matter in space, a process which would be like water running up a hill. Nor do they come to any appreciable amount from the stars. According to my investigations, the sun emits a radiation of such penetrative power that it is virtually impossible to absorb it in lead or other substances. ... This ray, which I call the primary solar ray, gives rise to a secondary radiation by impact against the cosmic dust scattered through space. It is the secondary radiation which now is commonly called the cosmic ray, and comes, of course, equally from all directions in space."

Nikola Tesla,
Serbian-American physicist
(1856–1943)

IT MAY SEEM OBVIOUS that a star as large, as hot, and as fuel rich as the sun would be a violent and highly combustible cosmic force. Though we observe the daily rising and setting of the sun, and witness occasional solar eclipses – these are only the most benign activities of our star. Upon closer inspection there exists an impressive and potentially catastrophic phenomena known as solar flares.

A solar flare is a sudden burst of magnetic energy within the sun's atmosphere (or corona) followed by a dramatic explosion called a coronal mass ejection (or CME). Only visible through a high-powered telescope, a CME is an immense flame of solar plasma, sometimes as large as a planet, reaching out like a fiery finger from the sun's corona and into space. Most common during times when the sun is highly active, these solar flares cause massive amounts of charged electrons to be emitted from the sun through the solar wind and into the rest of the solar system. The effects of such flares can greatly impact the Earth's magnetosphere and cripple electronic, navigational, and satellite capabilities on a massive intercontinental scale. Many scientists believe it is only a matter of time before we experience the impact of an active season of solar flares, known as a solar or geomagnetic storm.

"I am the LORD All-Powerful. I command the sun to give light each day, the moon and stars to shine at night, and ocean waves to roar."

Jeremiah 31:35 CEV

Extending above the photosphere or visible surface of the Sun , the faint, tenuous solar corona can't be easily seen from Earth, but it is measured to be hundreds of times hotter than the photosphere itself. What makes the solar corona so hot? Astronomers have long sought the source of the corona's heat in magnetic fields which loft monstrous loops of solar plasma above the photosphere. This tantalizing image shows clusters of the majestic, hot coronal loops which span 30 or more times the diameter of planet Earth.
NASA

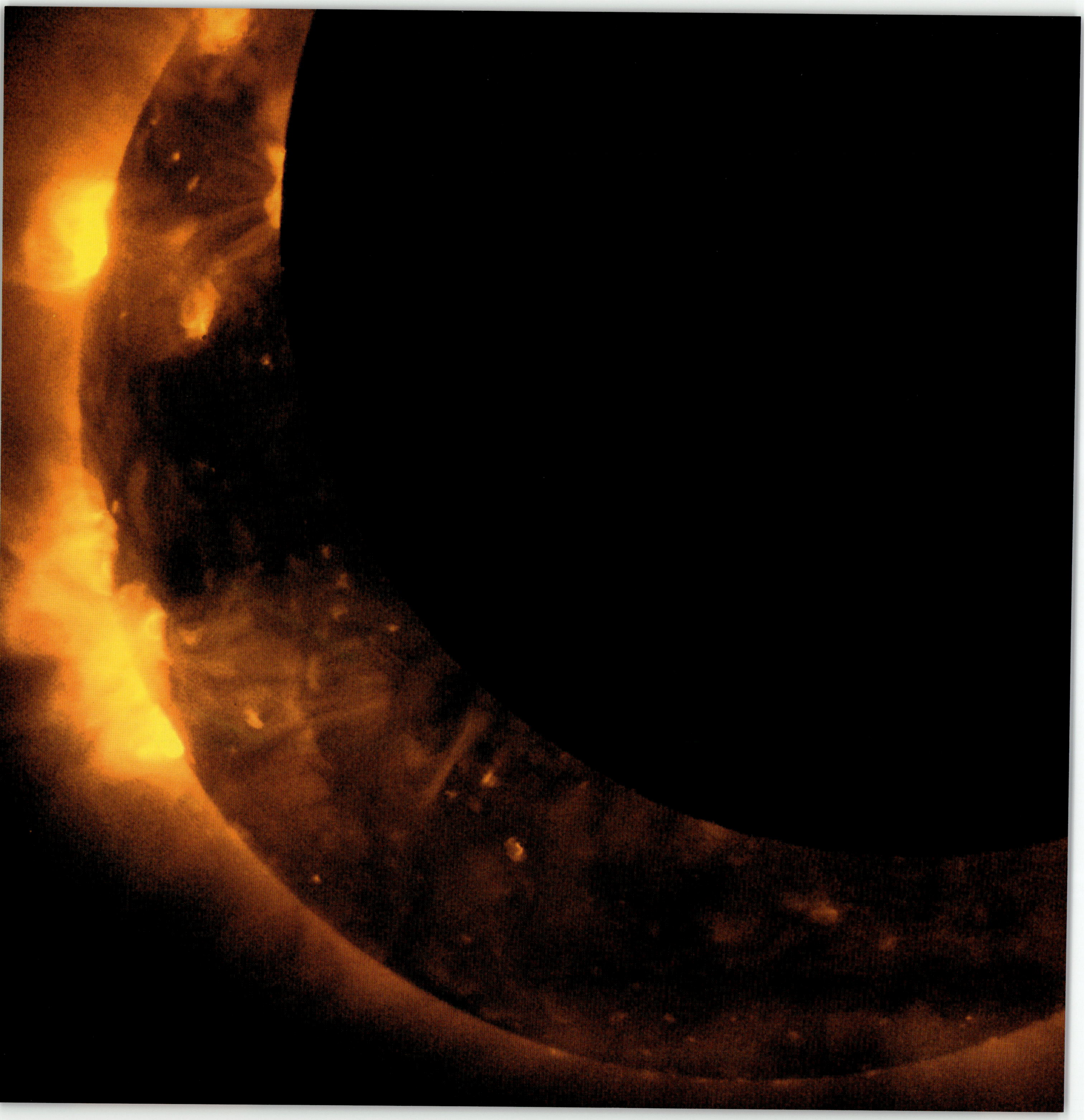

The Disappearing Sun

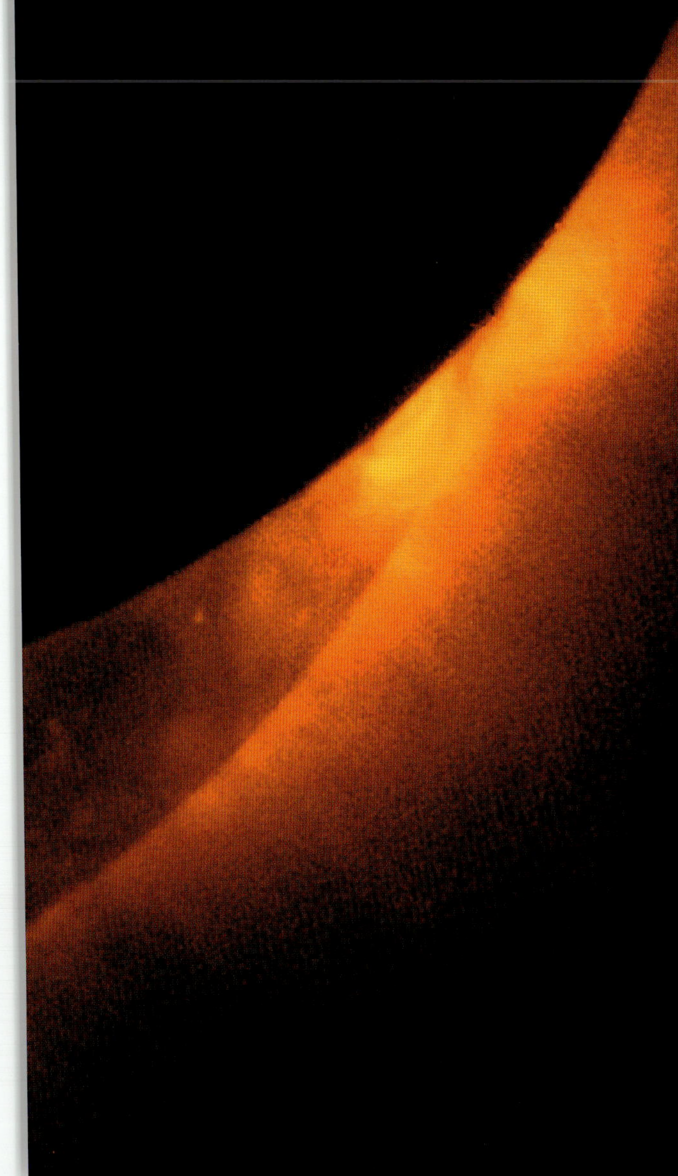

HOW TERRIFYING it must have been, a thousand or even just a few hundred years ago, to see the sun disappear in what we today know as an eclipse where the great light of day simply blacks out. It is no wonder that such occurrences were seen as omens, warnings, and messages from the "gods" of old.

First observed through telescopes in the 18th century, eclipses have taught scientists much about the alignment of bodies in space and, specifically, the sun's corona (or atmosphere) seen as a glowing "halo" during a total eclipse. A solar eclipse is possible even though the sun's diameter is approximately 400 times larger than the moon because the sun is roughly 400 times further away from Earth than the moon – thus creating the impression that the two bodies are the same size. This sun to moon ratio is also why, when a full moon passes directly in front of the daytime sun, it appears on Earth to obscure the sun. Lasting only a few minutes, solar eclipses are rare and only visible in the same geographic location every few hundred years, adding to their dramatic effect.

Even with our advanced knowledge of eclipses, this phenomena can seem "otherworldly" as the warm yellow glow of the the sun turns black, a reminder of the connected interplay happening in our solar system – a strange, predictable, but fascinating scene.

"On that day, I, the Lord God, will make the sun go down at noon, and I will turn daylight into darkness."

Amos 8:9 CEV
(Said to refer to the solar eclipse of June 15, 763 BC.)

"On the day of the new moon, in the month of Hiyar, the Sun was put to shame, and went down in the daytime, with Mars in attendance."

(One of the earliest written records of an eclipse of the Sun. Written on May 3, 1375 BC and found in the city of Ugarit in Mesopotamia.)

The Hinode spacecraft captured this image of the January 6, 2011, solar eclipse, which darkened the sky in parts of the Western United States and Southeast Asia yesterday. This image shows the maximum eclipse. HINODE/NASA

“Shout praises to the Lord! Everyone who serves him, come and praise his name. Let the name of the Lord be praised now and forever. From dawn until sunset the name of the Lord deserves to be praised. The Lord is far above all of the nations; he is more glorious than the heavens.”

Psalm 113:1-4 CEV

This is a Hubble Space Telescope image of a vast nebula called NGC 604. This is a site where new stars are being born in a spiral arm of the galaxy. At the heart of NGC 604 are over 200 hot stars, much more massive than our Sun (15 to 60 solar masses). They heat the gaseous walls of the nebula making the gas fluoresce. Their light also highlights the nebula's three-dimensional shape, like a lantern in a cavern. NASA

CHAPTER 4

OUR SOLAR SYSTEM

"The solar system has no anxiety about its reputation."

Ralph Waldo Emerson,
American poet and essayist (1803–1882)

"If we knew exactly what to expect throughout the solar system, we would have no reason to explore it."

Poul William Anderson,
The Saturn Game (1981)

"So I saw many planets, and they looked just a little bit brighter than they do from Earth."

Sally Ride,
American physicist and astronaut
(1951–2012)

Our Local Neighborhood

THE SUN is the center of our solar system, made up of a relatively small family of eight planets orbiting around the sun with their satellites or moons. The solar system is our cosmic neighborhood and our only natural laboratory in which astronomers and physicists seek to unravel the mysteries of the larger universe beyond. Among the billions of other planetary systems in the universe, our local system is minute. It is tucked away in a spiral arm somewhere in the Milky Way. Trying to locate it from outer space would be like looking for a needle in a haystack.

It wasn't until the 16th century that scientists realized the sun was the center of our planetary system. Until then the Ptolemaic system or geocentric model, the belief that the Earth is the orbital center of the sun and the other planets, was held to be true. But thanks to scientists like Copernicus, Galileo, and Kepler, a different theory called the heliocentric model gradually superceded Ptolemy's old theory.

Of the eight planets – Mercury, Venus, Earth, Mars, Jupiter, Saturn, Uranus, and Neptune – the four smaller inner planets or terrestrial planets of Mercury, Venus, Earth, and Mars are primarily composed of rock and metal, while the four outer planets or gas giants of Jupiter, Saturn, Uranus, and Neptune are much larger and more massive than the terrestrials. They are all held in place by the sun's enormous gravity pull and have almost circular orbits that lie within a nearly flat disc called the ecliptic plane.

Our solar system is remarkable for its very delicate balance needed to provide exactly the right conditions for planetary harmony and life on Earth. Its fine-tuning certainly provides prima facie evidence of deistic design.

"Planets move in ellipses with the sun at one focus."

Johannes Kepler, German astronomer (1571–1630)

"His glory covered the heavens and his praise filled the earth. His splendor was like the sunrise; rays flashed from his hand, where his power was hidden... His ways are eternal."

Habakkuk 3:3b-4,6b NIV

Facts About the Solar System

BODY	DIAMETER	DISTANCE FROM THE SUN	ORBITAL PERIOD	MOONS
The Sun	1,400,000 km (869,919 miles)			
The Moon	3,476 km (2,160 miles)	Distance from the Earth: 385,000 km (239,228 miles)		
Mercury	4,878 km (3,031miles)	58M km (36M miles)	88 days	0
Venus	12,104 km (7,521 miles)	108M km (67M miles)	224 days	0
The Earth	12,756 km (7,926 miles)	150M km (93M miles)	1 year	1
Mars	6,795 km (4,222 miles)	228M km (141M miles)	2 years	2
Jupiter	142,986 km (88,847 miles)	778M km (483M miles)	12 years	16+
Saturn	120,537 km (74,898 miles)	1,427M km (886M miles)	29 years	18+
Uranus	51,119 km (31,764 miles)	2,970M km (1,782M miles)	84 years	15+
Neptune	50,538 km (31,403 miles)	4,506M km (2,794M miles)	165 years	8+
(Pluto (dwarf)	2,274 km (1,413 miles)	5,913M km (3,666M miles)	246 years	5)

"Your love reaches higher than the heavens, and your loyalty extends beyond the clouds. Our God, may you be honored above the heavens; may your glory be seen everywhere on earth." Psalm 108:4-5 CEV

"The sun and its retinue of planets drift as a group through the vast gulfs of space that separate the stars."

Barney Oliver, founder and director of Hewlett Packard laboratories (1916–1995)

Mercury: Small and Swift

THE ANCIENT GREEKS mistook Mercury for two planets because of its swift orbit around the sun. So they named it twice. Apollo was one name. Hermes, their speedy messenger god, was the other. The Romans subsequently applied their adaptation of Hermes, which was Mercury, to the planet. The name stuck.

Indeed Mercury's revolution around the sun is a quick one at around 88 earth days, which is to be expected given its relatively short average distance from the sun, a mere 57.91 million km (35,983,606 miles). At such close range, surface temperatures on Mercury can reach over 400 degrees Celsius during the day and -180 degrees at night.

Because of its size (roughly 1/17 the size of the Earth) Mercury is difficult to spot and can best be seen in the sky at sunset and sunrise or as a tiny silhouette against the sun during a rare Mercury passage.

"Sing joyful songs to the Lord! Praise the mighty rock where we are safe. Come to worship him with thankful hearts and songs of praise. The Lord is the greatest God, king over all other gods."

Psalm 95:1-3 CEV

"I had rather be Mercury, the smallest among seven [planets], revolving round the sun, than the first among five [moons] revolving round Saturn."

Johann Wolfgang von Goethe (1749–1832)

This artist's rendition shows the Kepler-20 star system, where NASA's Kepler mission discovered the first Earth-size planets around a star beyond our own. The system is jam-packed with five planets, all circling within a distance roughly equivalent to Mercury's orbit in our solar system.

NASA/AMES/JPL-CALTECH

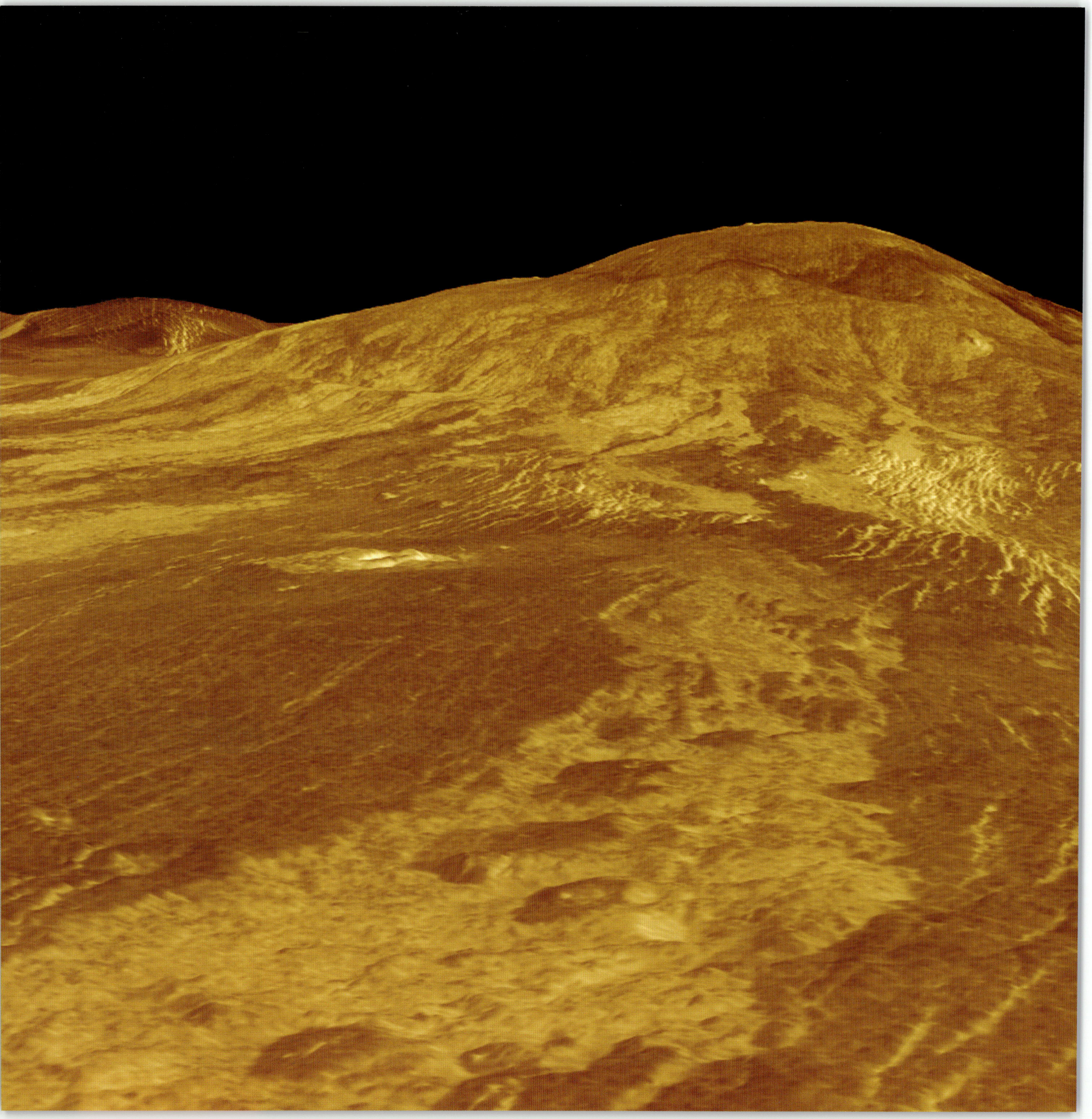

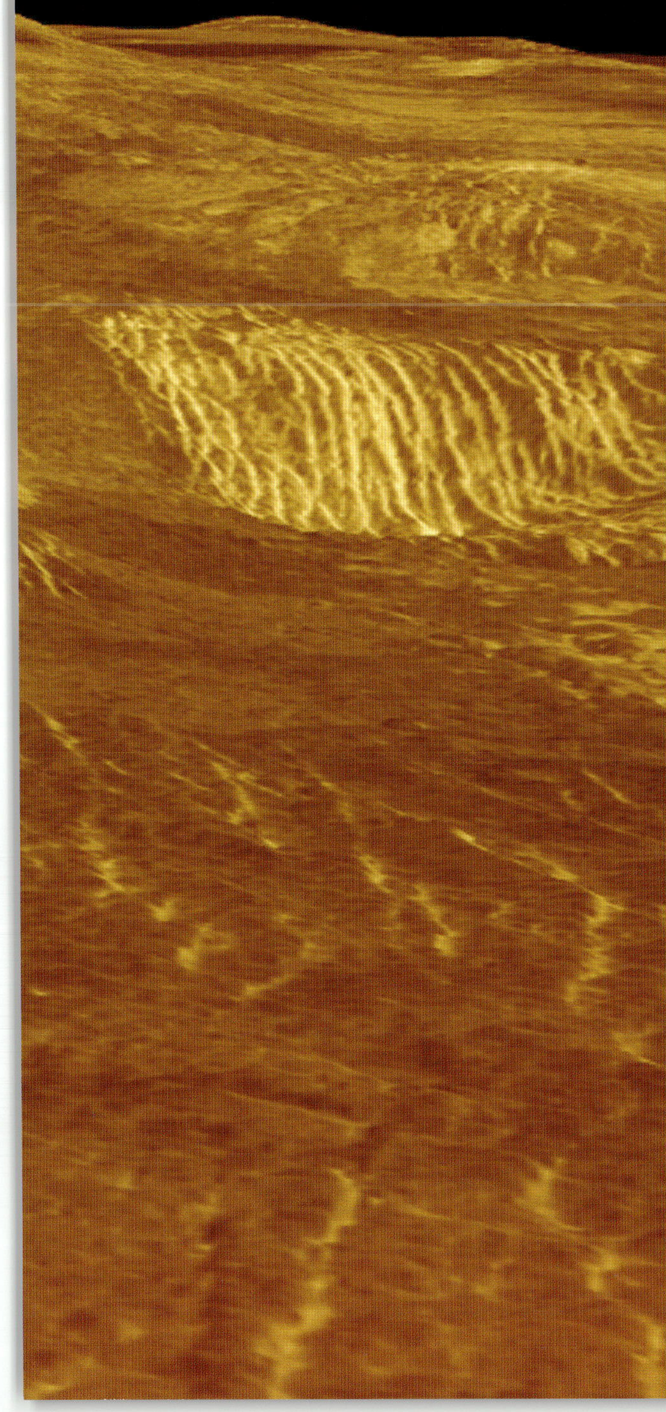

Venus: The Brilliant Planet

SHINING WHITE and pure like a pearl in the ocean of space, Venus is truly brilliant. Other than the moon and the sun, Venus is the brightest visible object in the night sky (as seen from Earth) and is often mistaken for a star.

Though it is the closest planet to Earth getting as near as 40 million km (24,854,848 miles), its proximity is not the primary reason for its high level of visibility. Venus actually owes its bright appearance to the fact that it is completely shrouded by clouds which reflect two-thirds of all the sunlight that reaches the planet creating its powerfully distinctive sheen. With such a prominent position in the sky, it is no wonder that the Romans named the planet after their goddess of beauty.

Yet the ivory veneer of Venus is only part of the story. Below the heavy cloud cover exists a lesser-known feature of the planet: its numerous volcanoes. Venus has, in fact, more volcanoes than any other planet or moon in the solar system. Night after night, since humans started looking into the sky, Venus has been a symbol of distant beauty, but only recently have we learned that underneath the beauty is a world of violence.

"O LORD, how manifold are your works! In wisdom have you made them all."

Psalm 104:24a ESV

"There are so many stars shining in the sky, so many beautiful things winking at you, but when Venus comes out, all the others are waned, they are pushed to the background."

Mehmet Murat Ildan (From the play *Galileo Galilei* (2001))

Sif Mons is displayed in this computer-simulated view of the surface of Venus. Lava flows extend for hundreds of kilometers across the fractured plains shown in the foreground to the base of Sif Mons. Sif Mons, a volcano with a diameter of 300 kilometers (186 miles) and a height of 2 kilometers (1.2 miles), appears in the upper half of the image. (Inset) The hemispheric view of Venus, as revealed by more than a decade of radar investigations culminating in the 1990-1994 Magellan mission. NASA/JPL/USGS

Mars: The Red Planet

DUE IN PART to its intense red color, Mars has certainly captivated our human imagination for centuries. In contrast to the calming blue and greens of Earth, Mars' orangey red calls to mind turmoil, passion, and conflict. Mars is a world of amber-colored discord.

The Red Planet has many interesting geological attributes. The most impressive is a volcanic peak (Olympus Mons) that rises almost 27 km (16.7 miles) above the surface. By comparison, three Mount Everests stacked

"I created the mountains and the wind. I let humans know what I am thinking. I bring darkness at dawn and step over hills. I am the Lord God All-Powerful!"

Amos 4:13 CEV

The planet Mars—crimson and bright, filling our telescopes with vague intimations of almost-familiar landforms—has long formed a celestial tabula rasa on which we have inscribed our planetological theories, utopian fantasies, and fears of alien invasion or ecological ruin.

David Grinspoon
(*Scientific American*, Nov. 2005)

upon each other would still not top the height of it. Another highlight of Mars' geology is a 4000 km (2,485 miles) long canyon system (Valles Marineris) that is wide enough to span the entire continental United States. These features are even more impressive when considering the scale, as the diameter of Mars measures only about half of that of Earth.

As debates continue about the viability of life ever existing on Mars, one thing is for certain – it is a harsh and dramatic planet with an average temperature of -63 degrees Celsius. Should any life form ever find its way to the Red Planet, it would have to contest with erupting volcanoes, endless canyons, minimal atmosphere, and raging planet-wide dust storms. But of course, such should be expected of a world named for a god of war.

The Twin Peaks are modest-size hills to the southwest of the Mars Pathfinder landing site. The peaks are approximately 30-35 meters (-100 feet) tall. North Twin is approximately 860 meters (2800 feet) from the lander, and South Twin is about a kilometer away (3300 feet). The scene includes bouldery ridges and swales or "hummocks" of flood debris that range from a few tens of meters away from the lander to the distance of the South Twin Peak. NASA/JPL

The Space Between

SOMETHING WAS MISSING.

If calculations by German astronomers Johann Titus and Johann Bode in 1772 were correct, then there was definitely something missing. But not just anything – an entire planet!

It was not that it was lost but, rather, that it was never found. The distance from Mars to Jupiter is around 547 million km (339,890,042 miles) on average. Titus and Bode concluded that that gap is too wide – there should be a planet in between. So when Giuseppi Piazzi in 1801 discovered the first asteroid of what we now know to be a large asteroid belt between Mars and Jupiter, it was more than noteworthy. Could these asteroids be remnants of a destroyed planet?

Whether the answer is yes or no, the belt does make a neat dividing line between the two classes of planets: the four terrestrial planets from Mercury to Mars on one side and the four gas giants from Jupiter to Neptune on the other.

The asteroid belt has an estimated one million asteroids between 1 and 25 km (15 million miles) in diameter. Because of constant collisions among these rocks, some are ejected from their orbit and captured by other planets to become moons.

"The truth is beyond us. It is far too deep."

Ecclesiastes 7:24 CEV

"When confronted with the order and beauty of the universe and the strange coincidences of nature, it's very tempting to take a leap of faith from science into religion. I am sure many physicists want to. I only wish they would admit it."

Tony Rothman, American theoretical physicist (1953–)

This artist's rendition illustrates a massive asteroid belt in orbit around a star the same age and size as our Sun. Asteroids are chunks of rock from "failed" planets, which never managed to coalesce into full-sized planets. Asteroid belts can be thought of as construction sites that accompany the building of rocky planets. NASA/JPL-CALTECH, , LUNAR AND PLANETARY INSTITUTE

Jupiter: The Mini System

JUPITER IS IN A CLASS of its own. As such, it can be instructive to study it alongside the sun. Indeed Jupiter and the sun have much in common. They are both composed primarily of hydrogen and helium, and just like the sun, Jupiter has several bodies in orbit around it. So far we have identified sixty-three moons in orbit around Jupiter.

Jupiter is the largest and most massive planet – 321 times bigger than Earth (over 1300 Earths could fit inside of it). In addition, Jupiter's mass is two and a half times that of all the other planets combined. Yet compared with the sun, Jupiter is a pebble. More than 900 Jupiters could fit inside the sun. Yes, Jupiter is unique – bigger than the other planets yet too small to be a star.

"No one can ever build a temple large enough for God—even the heavens are too small a place for him to live in!"

2 Chronicles 2:6 CEV

The NASA/ESA Hubble Space Telescope has caught Jupiter's moon Ganymede playing a game of "peek-a-boo." NASA, ESA AND E. KARKOSCHKA (UNIVERSITY OF ARIZONA)

"Poets say science takes away from the beauty of the stars – mere globs of gas atoms. Nothing is "mere." I too can see the stars on a desert night, and feel them. But do I see less or more? The vastness of the heavens stretches my imagination – stuck on this carousel my little eye can catch one-million-year-old light. A vast pattern – of which I am a part... What is the pattern or the meaning or the why? It does not do harm to the mystery to know a little more about it. For far more marvelous is the truth than any artists of the past imagined it. Why do the poets of the present not speak of it? What men are poets who can speak of Jupiter if he were a man, but if he is an immense spinning sphere of methane and ammonia must be silent?"

Richard Freyman, American physicist (1918–1988)

Saturn: The Ringed Planet

ANY DISCUSSION OF SATURN begins with its rings. Though the other three gas giants, Jupiter, Uranus, and Neptune, have rings of their own, none are as bright or beautiful as Saturn's, easily making it the most recognizable planet.

How many rings does Saturn have? This is a hard question to answer. The rings are designated letters in the order of their discovery, but each one is actually a system of thousands of smaller rings, making it difficult to determine their exact quantity. Besides that, a ring of Saturn is not one contiguous mass (like a solid sheet of ice) as it might appear from a distance. On the contrary, fragmented particles up to the size of an automobile make up each ring.

Comprised mostly of ice, these rings are remarkably thin – only sixty feet thick compared to a diameter of 290,000 km (180,198 miles). Because of this extreme thinness and in combination with the tilt of the planet, there are times when the rings are completely invisible from earth. But when visible they look razor sharp as if they were threatening to slice through anything in their orbital path. Add to this the planet's speedy axial rotation (10.23 hours), and Saturn is like the solar system's own buzzsaw, both spectacular and dangerous.

"I still remember when the first time I pointed the telescope at the sky and I saw Saturn with the rings. It was a beautiful image."

Umberto Guidoni, Italian politician and former ESA astronaut (1954–)

"He loves justice and fairness, and he is kind to everyone everywhere on earth. The Lord made the heavens and everything in them by his word."

Psalm 33:5-6 CEV

Saturn's atmosphere and its rings are shown here in a false-color composite. Red and orange colors in this view indicate clouds that are deep in the atmosphere. Yellow and green colors, most noticeable along the top edge of the view, indicate intermediate clouds. White and blue indicate high clouds and haze. The rings appear as a thin horizontal line of bright blue because they are outside of the atmosphere and not affected by methane absorption.

NASA/JPL-CALTECH/SPACE SCIENCE INSTITUTE

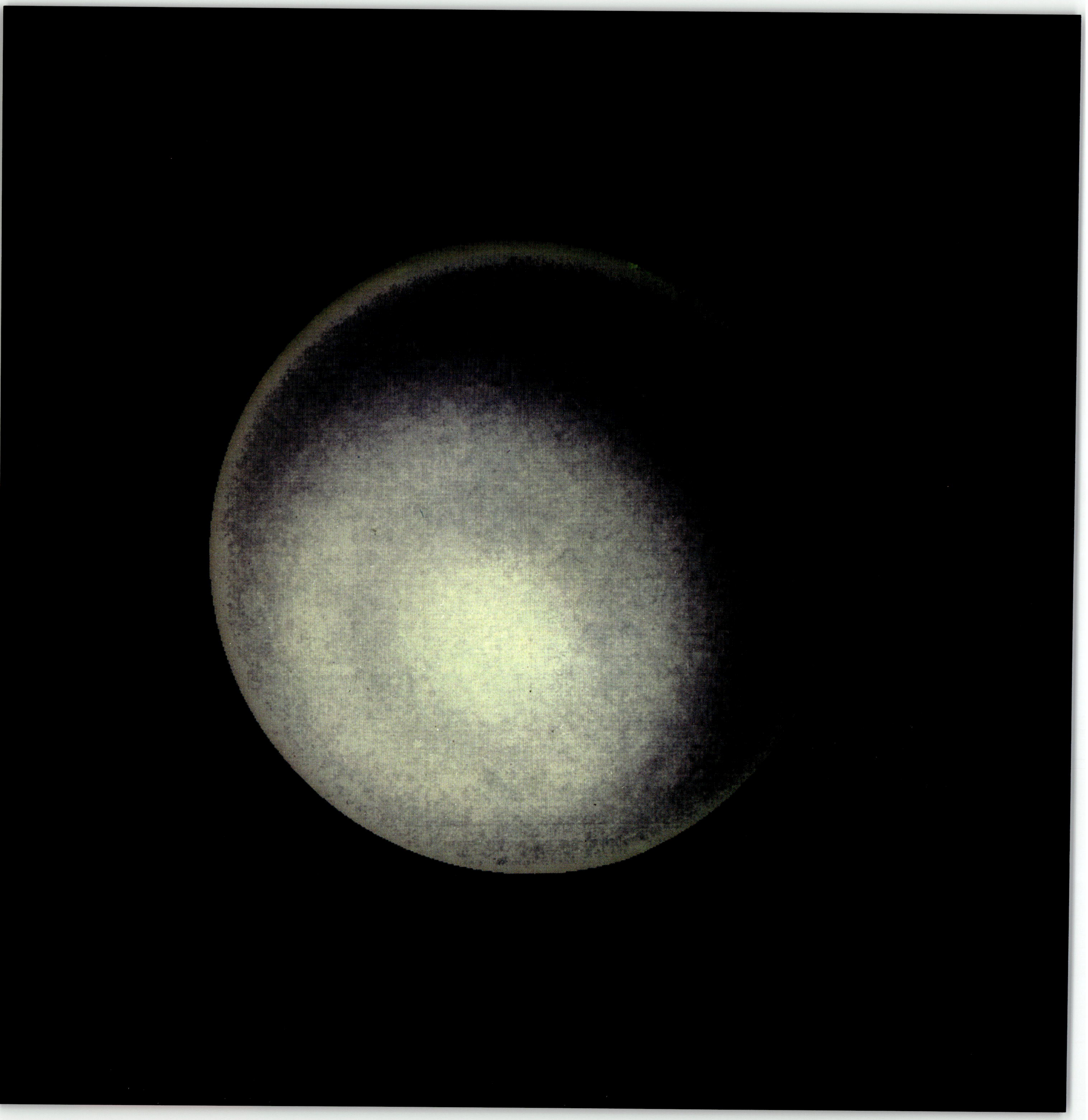

Uranus: The Misfit Planet

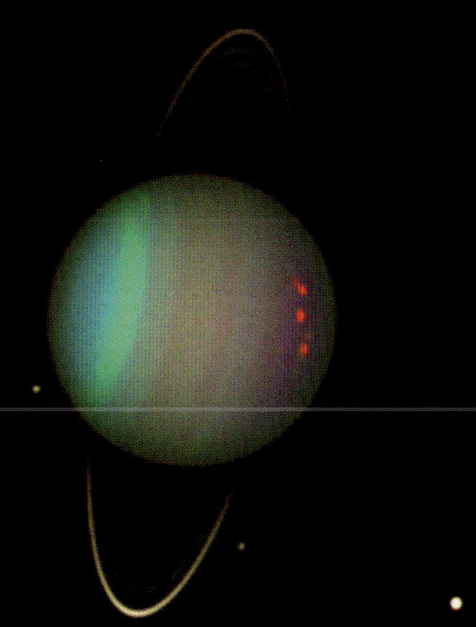

(Above) *This wider view of Uranus reveals the planet's faint rings and several of its satellites. The outermost ring is made of dust and small pebbles, which create a thin, dark, and almost vertical line across the right side of Uranus. The bright satellite on the lower right corner is Ariel, which has a snowy white surface. Five small satellites with dark surfaces can be seen just outside the rings. Clockwise from the top, they are: Desdemona, Belinda, Portia, Cressida and Puck.* (Facing page) *This computer enhancement emphasizes the high-level haze in Uranus' upper atmosphere. Clouds are obscured by the overlying atmosphere.* NASA/JPL/USGS/ESA AND ERICH KARKOSCHKA, UNIVERSITY OF ARIZONA

URANUS WAS THE FIRST PLANET to be discovered through an amateur telescope in 1781. Yet we didn't know much about this planet until Voyager 2 flew by in January 1986.

At first glance, Uranus seems quite boring when compared to the other seven planets. Were Uranus an emotional being, it might be prone to envy – it even has a greenish tint!

Yet when you take a closer look, you will find Uranus is far from boring. In fact, this blue-green gas giant that is four times the size of the Earth has its own superlative that just might be more interesting – if less obvious – than the rest of the planets. Uranus has an axial tilt of nearly ninety-eight degrees. What this means is that the planet essentially lies on its side, spinning perpendicular to its path of orbit around the sun. Combining its tilt with the fact that its revolution lasts 84 years means that each pole takes turns spending 42 years in utter darkness.

In the midst of these extremes, Uranus does have one boast besides its family of 27 moons. Due to the planet's awkward angle, the sun can be directly overhead at every single latitude at least once during its revolution. No other planet can claim that.

"God stretches the northern sky over empty space and hangs the earth on nothing."

Job 26:7 NIV

"For a long time, we've worked on detecting planets with whatever was at hand, making use of existing small telescopes or even amateur telescopes. It's time to move on to the next stage."

Andrew Gould,
former chairman and
chief executive officer of
Schlumberger (1946–)

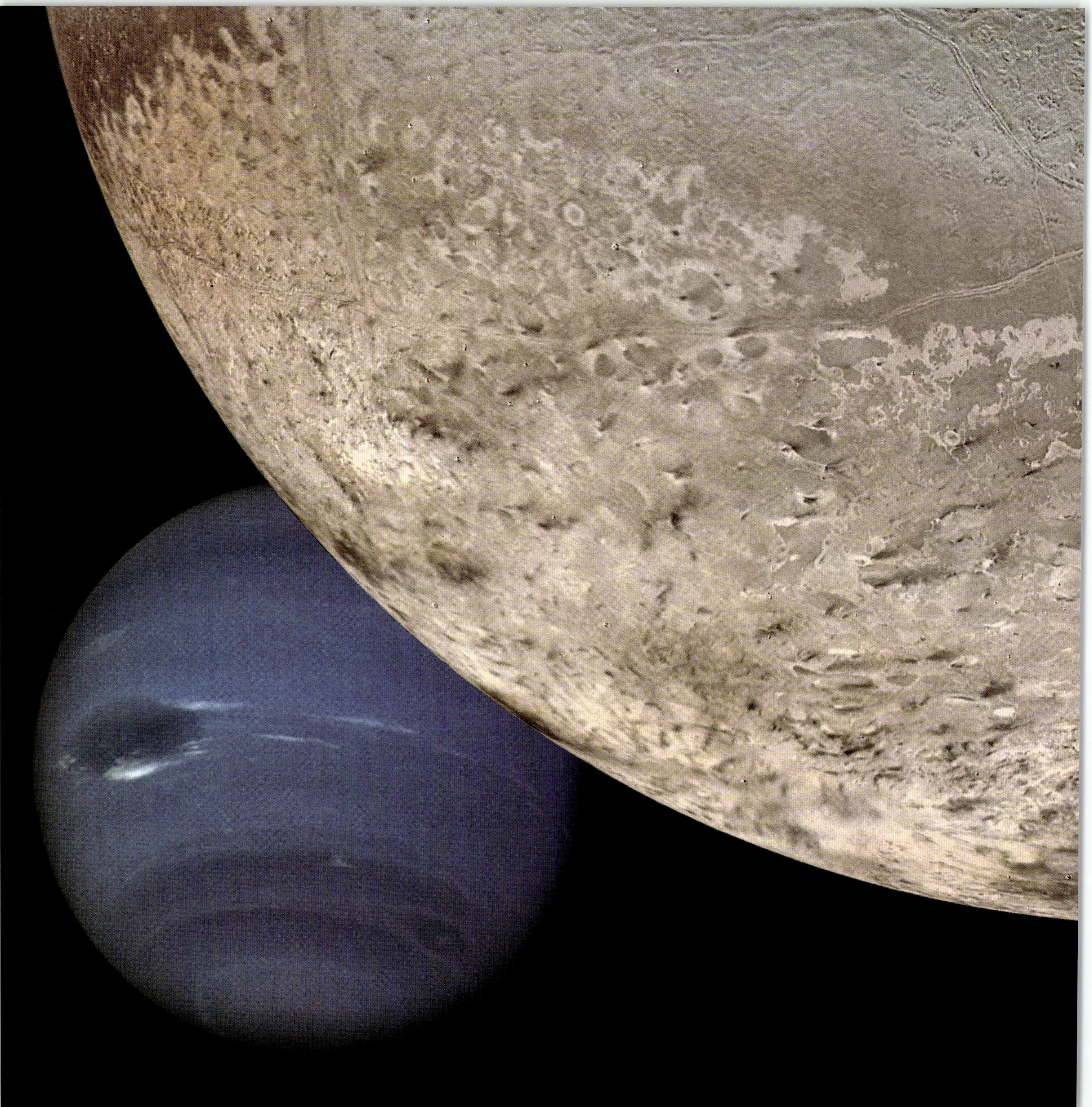

Neptune: The Other Blue Planet

NEPTUNE IS THE PLANET farthest away from the sun (4.5 billion km or 2.8 billion miles) – so far away that it takes 165 years for it to travel its 4.5 million km circuit around the sun. It is extremely dark and cold (below -221 degrees Celsius at the surface clouds). As the outlier of the planets, Neptune cannot be seen by the naked eye because it is so far removed from a light source. What we know about this inhospitable planet is mainly due to Voyager 2 that flew by it in 1989 and took the photos shown on this page.

Neptune rolls along this remote path, a serene orbiting blue marble with white swirls. But any perceived peacefulness is pure illusion. Neptune has the swiftest winds in the solar system at 2,400 km/h (1500 miles/hour). By comparison, Earth's speediest gusts reach 368 km/h (230 mph).

At the edge of space Neptune travels as an isolated, cold, dark, and blustery ball of gas far removed from all that we associate with the heat and light of life.

"The Voyager mission has opened up our solar system in a way not possible before the Space Age... It revealed our neighbors in the outer solar system and showed us how much there is to learn and how diverse the bodies are that share the solar system with our own planet Earth."

Dr. Edward C. Stone, Voyager Project Scientist (1972–)

"'Can anyone hide in secret places so that I cannot see him?' declares the LORD. 'Do not I fill heaven and earth?' declares the LORD."

Jeremiah 23:24 NIV

This computer-generated montage shows Neptune as it would appear from a spacecraft approaching Triton, Neptune's largest moon at 2706 km (1683 mi) in diameter. Triton's surface is mostly covered by nitrogen frost mixed with traces of condensed methane, carbon dioxide, and carbon monoxide. The tenuous atmosphere of Triton, though only about one-hundredth of one percent of Earth's atmospheric density at the surface, is thick enough to produce wind-deposited streaks of dark and bright materials of unknown composition in the south polar cap region. NASA/JPL/USGS

Pluto: The Unapologetic Dwarf

IN 2006 the International Astronomical Union demoted Pluto from planet status to dwarf planet. And yet, the tiny distant dwarf stubbornly continues on its odd orbit refusing to apologize for what it is.

And like any good outcast, Pluto is a rebel. Relatively speaking, Pluto's 2,400 km (1,491 miles) diameter is tiny. Pluto also follows an odd orbital path. While the eight official planets more or less stay on the same general plane, Pluto's path takes a much more extreme angle tilted about 20 degrees. This tilt accounts for its temporary place swap with Neptune. No other planet crosses another's path of orbit. Another oddity about Pluto is its axial rotation. For some of its year, the sun rises in the south and sets in the north. But despite its small stature, Pluto does have at least five moons, while Mercury and Venus have none.

Planet or not, the fact that an object around 6 billion km (3,7 billion miles) from the center of the solar system would still be in orbit demonstrates the impressive pull that the Sun has – not to mention the determination of the little dwarf planet to hang on.

"With the Lord a day is like a thousand years, and a thousand years are like a day."

2 Peter 3:8 NIV

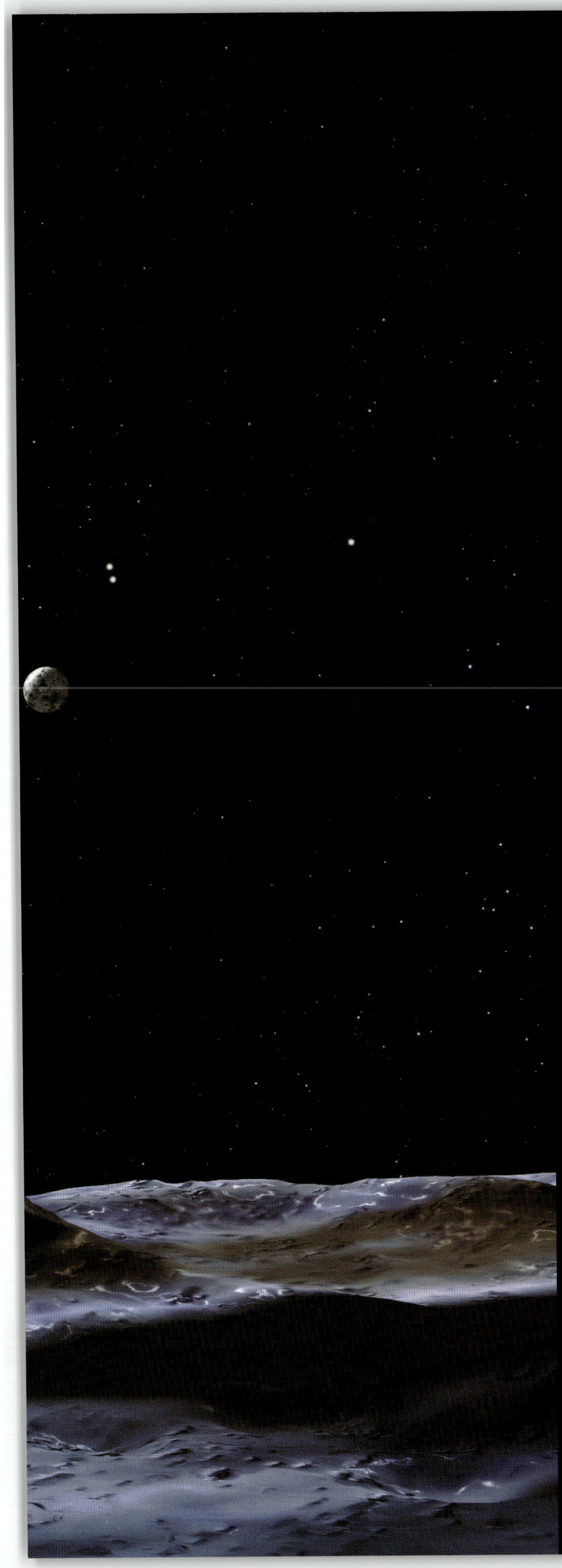

The artist's concept shows the Pluto system from the surface of one of the candidate moons. The other members of the Pluto system are just above the moon's surface. Pluto is the large disk at center, right. Charon, the system's only confirmed moon, is the smaller disk to the right of Pluto. The other candidate moon is the bright dot on Pluto's far left. NASA, ESA AND G. BACON (STSCI)

"Pluto is only about twice the size of Charon, so if you put Pluto and Charon on the cosmic seesaw, you would find that the balance point is a little bit outside Pluto rather than inside it. Again, there is nothing particularly special going on there. If you were to find yourself at that precise spot, you would only notice that you were very, very cold and could no longer breathe."

Mike Brown, *How I Killed Pluto* (2010)

CHAPTER 5

THE STARS

"He made the bright lights in the sky. God's love never fails. He lets the sun rule each day. God's love never fails. He lets the moon and the stars rule each night. God's love never fails." Psalm 136:7-9 CEV

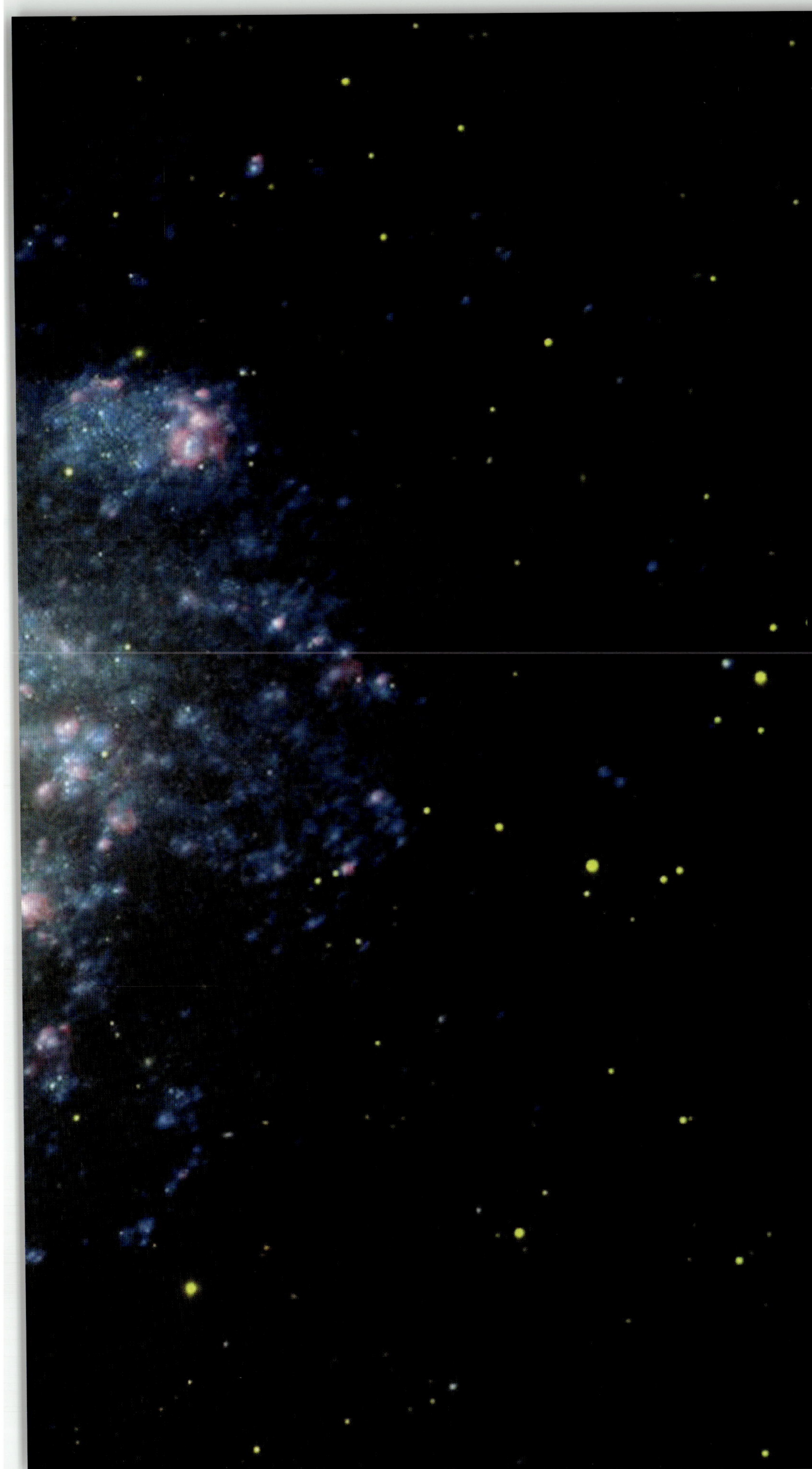

This graphic contains an image and illustration of a nearby star, named CoRoT-2a, which has a planet in close orbit around it. (Facing page) This composite image traces star formation in progress. Young hot blue stars dominate the outer spiral arms of the galaxy, while the older stars congregate in the nuclear regions which appear yellow-green. Gases heated by hot young stars and shocks due to winds from massive stars and supernova explosions appear in pink, as revealed by the visible-light image of the galaxy.
NASA/JPL-CALTECH/OCIW

What is A Star?

LOOKING UP AT NIGHT, the stars above us appear as thousands of tiny lights against the black sky of space – sometimes blinking, sometimes imagined as connected visions of mythic characters. The stars have always been poetic, inspiring stories and guiding sailors. And yet, upon closer inspection, scientists have found that all the multitude of stars in our galaxy are actually brightly burning masses of dust and gasses. Though they appear relatively close to one another when we view them as constellations, the stars themselves are light years apart from each other and from Earth. Within the Milky Way galaxy alone, there are hundreds of billions of stars infinite in their variety and relation to one another. There are stars of all shapes and ages and colors and sizes. If we imagine the sun as being the size of a large melon, then the relative sizes of other stars can range from that of a blueberry all the way up to the size of a skyscraper.

Like everything in creation, the stars have an order to their existence. They are born, they live, and, as supernovas and nebulae, they die.

"God made two powerful lights, the brighter one to rule the day and the other to rule the night. He also made the stars."

Genesis 1:16 CEV

"Men love to wonder, and that is the seed of science."

Ralph Waldo Emerson,
American poet and essayist
(1803–1882)

Hubble's view of the Carina Nebula shows star birth in a new level of detail. The fantasy-like landscape of the nebula is sculpted by the action of outflowing winds and scorching ultraviolet radiation from the monster stars that inhabit this inferno. In the process, these stars are shredding the surrounding material that is the last vestige of the giant cloud from which the stars were born. NASA

The Color of Stars

THOUGH IT MAY APPEAR upon first glance that all stars are the same color, they are almost as varied in hue as the colors of a rainbow.

The color of a star is directly related to its surface temperature. But for stellar purposes, the term "red hot" does not apply. Red stars are actually the coolest stars, averaging less than 4,000 degrees Celsius (less than 7,000 degrees F), while blue stars are the hottest at 45,000 degrees C (80,000 degrees F). Yellow stars like the sun lie somewhere in the middle. White dwarfs are the exception to this rule. They lie all over the temperature spectrum because they start out very hot and quickly cool down.

A star that burns hydrogen in its core is referred to as a "main sequence star." In general these are the yellow, blue, and bluish-white stars. Ninety percent of the visible stars are main sequence stars, but some of the brightest in the sky, such as Polux, have ceased burning hydrogen. As a star runs out of hydrogen and exits the main sequence, it transitions into a red giant (for all but the most massive stars) and eventually turns into a white dwarf.

Such a wide color spectrum is only visible through a telescope but again underlines the beautiful variety of even the most distant details of creation.

"What supports the foundation? Who placed the cornerstone, while morning stars sang, and angels rejoiced?" Job 38:6-7 CEV

"A hundred years ago, Auguste Compte, … a great philosopher, said that humans will never be able to visit the stars, that we will never know what stars are made out of, that that's the one thing that science will never ever understand because they're so far away. And then, just a few years later, scientists took starlight, ran it through a prism, looked at the rainbow coming from the starlight, and said, 'Hydrogen!'"

Michio Kaku, American theoretical physicist (1947–)

This image from the NASA/ESA Hubble Space Telescope shows Sh 2-106, or S106 for short. This is a compact star forming region in the constellation Cygnus (The Swan). A newly formed star called S106 IR is shrouded in dust at the centre of the image, and is responsible for the surrounding gas cloud's hourglass-like shape and the turbulence visible within. Light from glowing hydrogen is coloured blue in this image. NASA

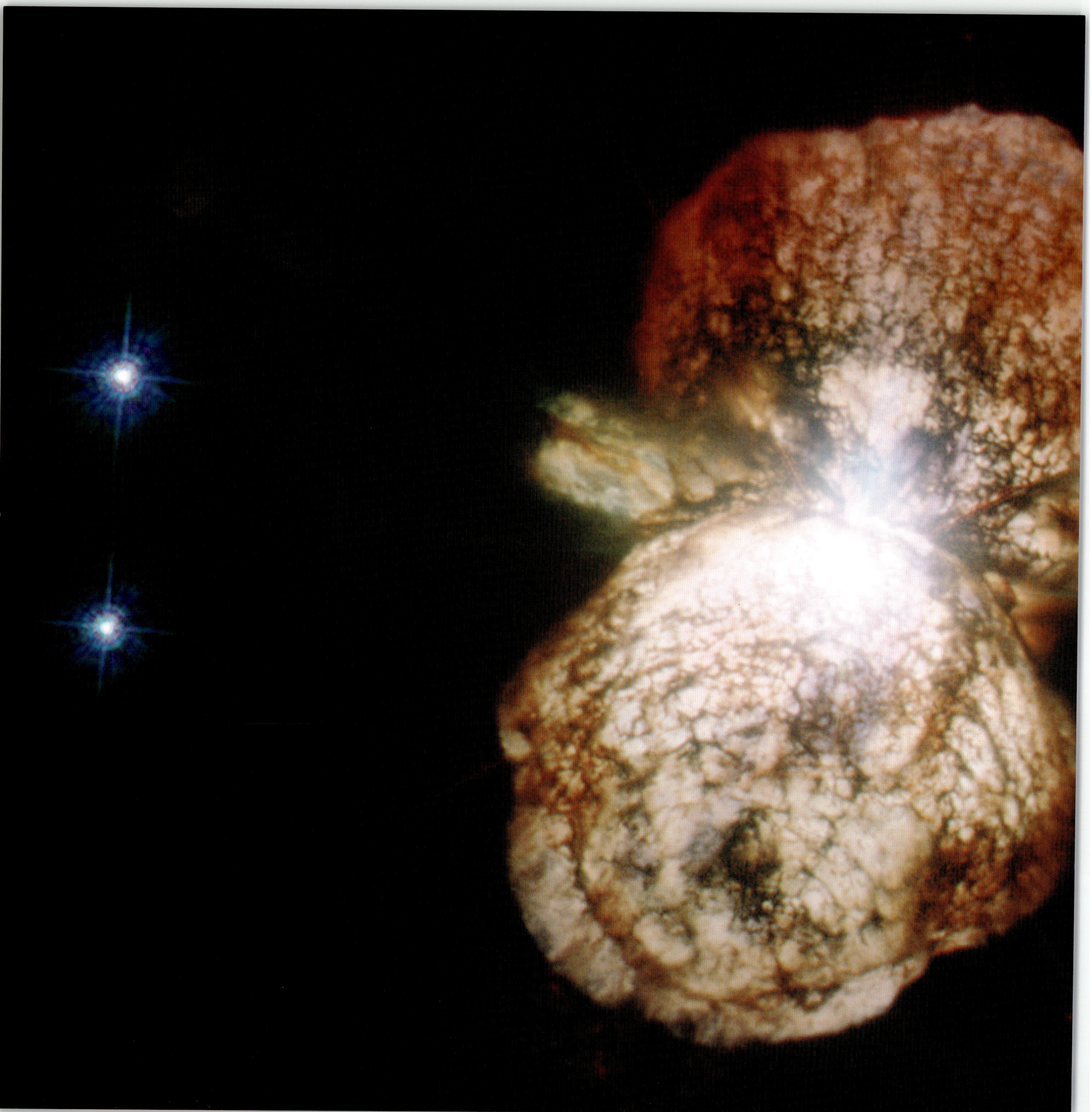

Supernovas

STARS CLASSIFIED as Red Supergiants can be up to ten times greater in size than the sun. A defining quality of the supergiant is the way that it collapses and dies after burning through its hydrogen fuel. One huge star located in our galaxy is Eta Carinae only 7,500 light years away. This monster star has a radius 400 times the size of the sun and luminosity about five million times that of the sun.

But that's nothing compared to the largest known star – the red hypergiant VY Canis Majoris, located almost 5,000 light years away. This star is calculated by most astronomers to be more than 2,100 times the size of our sun, which amounts to one third of the size of our entire solar system. At the speed of 900 km/h (560 miles/hour), it would take an airplane over 1,100 years to circle it once. Some astronomers disagree, claiming that VY Canis Majoris is probably only 600 times the size of the sun.

As the energy of a collapsing supergiant star builds and succumbs to the forces of gravity, the center of the star implodes, and the result is called a supernova. The spectacular nuclear reactions of a supernova can fill a star's home galaxy with an incredible display of brilliant color and light like silent interstellar fireworks exploding for the fortunate observer to witness. Eta Carinae might explode pretty soon into one of the most spectacular supernovas humans have ever seen.

If the living stars are reminders of God as a guide in times of darkness, the death of supergiant stars are reminders of His infinite grandeur and limitless luminosity.

"How is it they live in such harmony the billions of stars - when most men can barely go a minute without declaring war in their minds about someone they know."

St. Thomas Aquinas

"Sun and moon, and all of you bright stars, come and offer praise."

Psalm 148:3 CEV

At the turn of the 19th century, the binary star system Eta Carinae was faint and undistinguished. In the first decades of the century, it became brighter and brighter, until, by April 1843, it was the second brightest star in the sky, outshone only by Sirius (which is almost a thousand times closer to Earth). In the years that followed, it gradually dimmed again and by the 20th century was totally invisible to the naked eye.

Eta Carinae is not only interesting because of its past, but also because of its future. It is one of the closest stars to Earth that is likely to explode in a supernova in the relatively near future (though in astronomical timescales the "near future" could still be a million years away). When it does, expect an impressive view from Earth, far brighter still than its last outburst: SN 2006gy, the brightest supernova ever observed, came from a star of the same type. NASA

Binary Stars

TAKE A LOOK AT THE SKY on a cloudless night, and what do you see? Thousands upon thousands of tiny bright lights shining in the heavens. While some of these lights are other objects – nebulae, planets, even galaxies, most are stars. Yet even though the stars are countless, there are still more than you might think. The majority of stars are part of a binary system, meaning each star you see actually could be two stars in one.

A binary system then is simply two stars that orbit each other. The pair are often formed around the same time and place and latch on to each other like siblings in the sky. While some binary stars are far enough apart that we can see them as separate, many appear as one for various reasons. They are too close to each other or too far away for us to differentiate, or one of the stars is very dim and therefore not visible.

But if we cannot see the second star, how do we know it is there? Even if the star is not detectable telescopically or by other technological means, the irregular movement/path of the pair is a dead giveaway since binaries typically perform a bit of a drunken dance as they orbit about in the universe. Imagine trying to run around a track while spinning in circles, and you get the idea.

"Who can count his army of stars? Isn't God the source of light?"

Job 25:3 CEV

"Put three grains of sand inside a vast cathedral, and the cathedral will be more closely packed with sand than space is with stars."

Sir James Jeans, British astronomer and physicist (1877–1946)

This artist concept depicts a quadruple-star system called HD 98800. The system is approximately 10 million years old, and is located 150 light-years away in the constellation TW Hydrae. HD 98800 contains four stars, which are paired off into doublets, or binaries. The stars in the binary pairs orbit around each other, and the two pairs also circle each other like choreographed ballerinas. NASA/JPL-CALTECH/UCLA

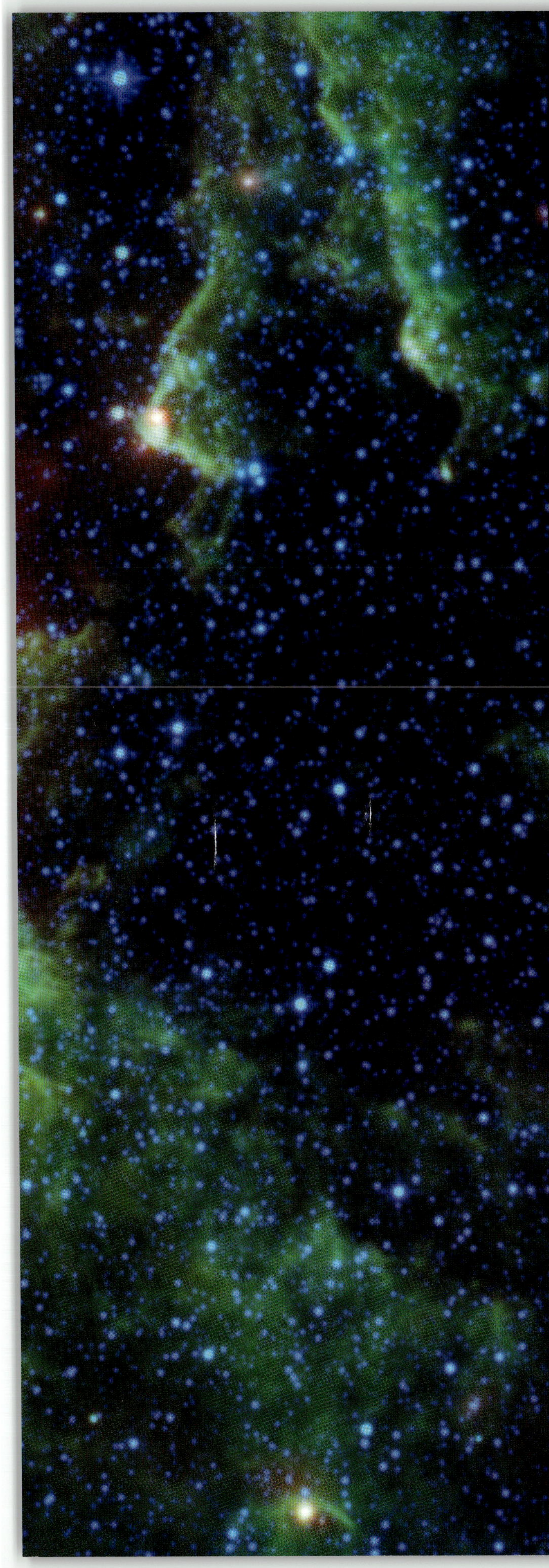

Alpha Centauri, The Nearest of Stars

ALPHA CENTAURI is the nearest star system to the sun at just over 4 light years away. That might seem close until you do the math and realize that 4 light years is more than 40 trillion km (about 24 trillion miles). True, compared to other objects like galaxies that lie millions of light years away, Alpha Centauri is close.

At such a distance, the binary stars, Alpha Centauri A and B, take about 80 years to complete an orbit around one another. Centauri A, the brighter of the two, is similar to the sun in many ways, particularly its size (only about 10% larger than the sun).

The third star in the system, aptly named Proxima Centauri, is actually the closest of all known stars to our sun. Despite this fact, Proxima is invisible without instrumentation due to its status as a red dwarf. Yet taken together, Alpha Centauri is the third brightest star in the sky.

"You alone are the LORD, Creator of the heavens and all the stars, Creator of the earth and those who live on it, Creator of the ocean and all its creatures. You are the source of life, praised by the stars that fill the heavens."

Nehemiah 9:6 CEV

"The very closest stars would require many years to visit, even traveling at the speed of light, which is impossible according to Einstein's theory of relativity. Today's fastest spaceships would require 200,000 years to travel to Alpha Centauri, our closest bright star. The energy required to send a hundred colonists to another star, as Frank Drake has pointed out, would be enough to meet the energy needs of the entire United States over a human lifetime. And these estimates are regarding nearby stars. When we consider the distances across the entire galaxy, and between galaxies, interstellar travel seems absolutely untenable."

David E. Fischer, American geochemist (1932–)

This infrared image shows the Lambda Centauri nebula, a star-forming cloud in our Milky Way galaxy, also known as the Running Chicken nebula. The nebula is about 5,800 light-years from Earth and is home to a new cluster of stars born from the cloud nearly 8 million years ago.

NASA/JPL-CALTECH/UCLA

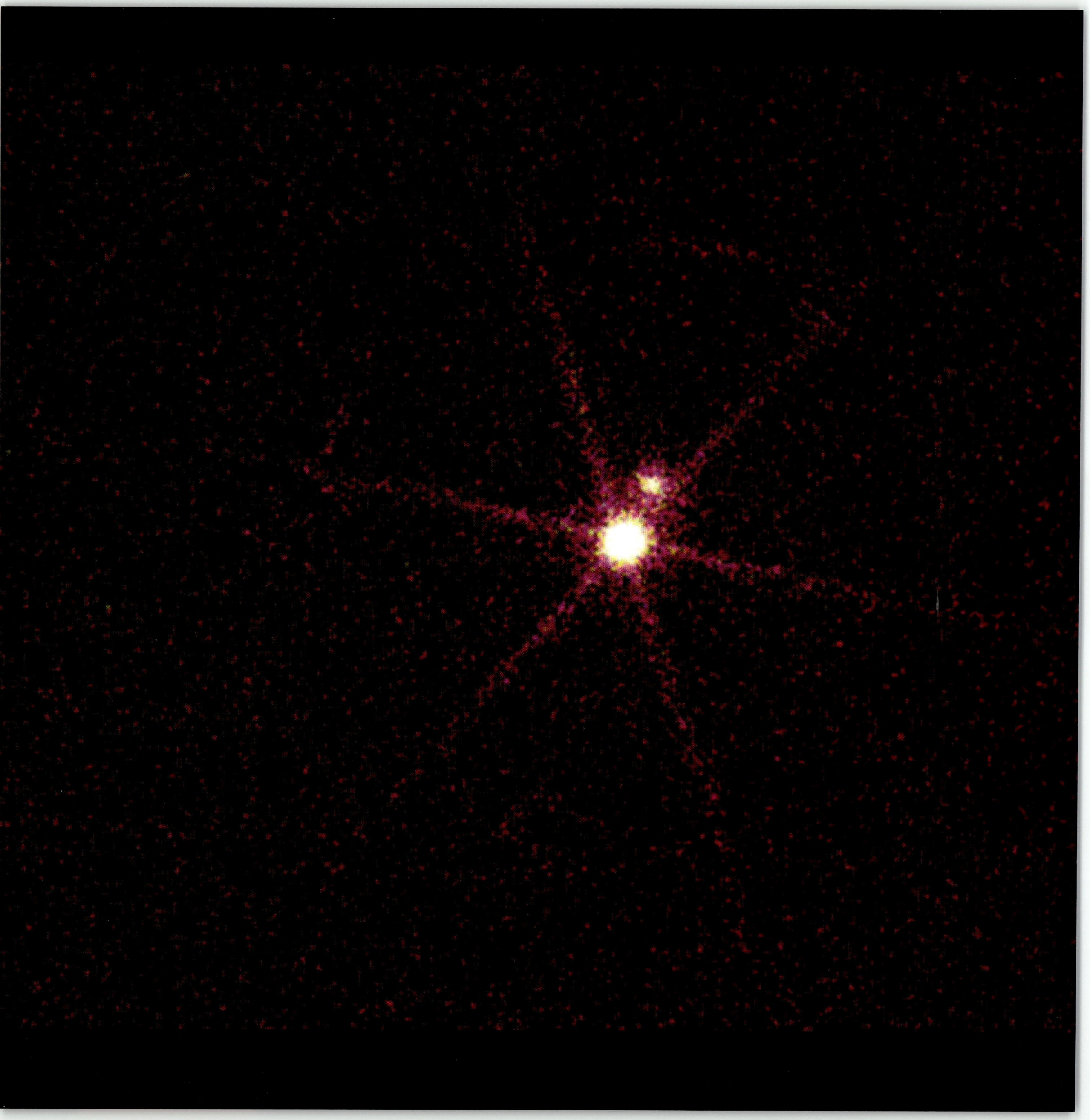

The Dog Star

"Sirius, the brightest star in the heavens... My grandfather would say we're part of something incredibly wonderful – more marvelous than we imagine. My grandfather would say we ought to go out and look at it once in a while so we don't lose our place in it."

Robert Fulghum, American author (1937–)

SIRIUS IS THE BRIGHTEST star in the sky even though it is twice as far from our solar system as Alpha Centauri. Take a look at the stars during winter months in either hemisphere, and you will see it near Orion's Belt. It lies amid the Canis Major constellation – accounting for its nickname, "The Dog Star." The word Sirius is Greek and means "scorching" or "glowing" that alludes to its brightness.

Sirius would outshine the sun by 25 times were they the same distance away from us. But even at its great distance, it is almost twice as bright as the next brightest star in the sky, Canopus.

As with many stars when you gaze upon Sirius, you are actually looking at not one but two stars. The binary's components are Sirius A, a white main sequence star, and Sirius B, a white dwarf. The latter gets little credit because it is always compared to A. Though much tinier, Sirius B has the mass of our sun but is compacted into a smaller size than Earth. The two make an interesting couple. B, nearing the end of its life, recalls its former glory while A shines on proudly, oblivious to its future fate.

"But the LORD created the stars and put them in place. He turns darkness to dawn and daylight to darkness; he scoops up the ocean and empties it on the earth."

Amos 5:8 CEV

An X-ray image of the Sirius star system located 8.6 light years from Earth. This image shows two sources and a spike-like pattern due to the support structure for the transmission grating. The bright source is Sirius B, a white dwarf star that has a surface temperature of about 25,000 ° Celsius which produces very low energy X-rays. The dim source at the position of Sirius A – a normal star more than twice as massive as the Sun – may be due to ultraviolet radiation from Sirius A leaking through the filter on the detector.

In contrast, Sirius A is the brightest star in the northern sky when viewed with an optical telescope, while Sirius B is 10,000 times dimmer. Because the two stars are so close together Sirius B escaped detection until 1862 when Alvan Clark discovered it while testing one of the best optical telescopes in the world at that time. NASA/SAO/CXC

Betelgeuse

OF ALL THE CONSTELLATIONS in the sky, Orion the Hunter is probably the most recognizable due to its large number of bright stars, its visibility in both hemispheres, and its distinctive three-star "belt." But while the belt gets the most attention, there is a lesser-known star in Orion's constellation that is no less interesting.

This star is called Betelgeuse and is found in the shoulder of the constellation Orion. The name from Arabic origin is pronounced "Beetlejuice." Also known as Alpha Orionis, Betelgeuse is a variable star, which means its brightness varies as much as one magnitude, occasionally outshining Rigel, generally the brightest in the constellation.

Betelgeuse is a red supergiant that lies about 425 light years away. Its diameter is over 1000 times greater than that of the sun, making it one of the largest known stars. Were the star in place of the sun, it would stretch all the way to the Asteroid Belt, engulfing Mercury, Venus, Earth, and Mars. Yet, Betelgeuse is "only" half the size of VY Canis Majoris.

"God alone stretched out the sky, stepped on the sea, and set the stars in place—the Big Dipper and Orion, the Pleiades and the stars in the southern sky. Of all the miracles God works, we cannot understand a one." Job 9:7-10 CEV

"I have looked further into space than ever a human being did before me. I have observed stars of which the light, it can be proved, must take two million years to reach the earth."

Sir William Herschel, German-British astronomer (1738–1822)

Polaris, The North Star

"And when you look up to the sky and see the sun, the moon and the stars—all the heavenly array—do not be enticed into bowing down to them and worshiping things the Lord your God has apportioned to all the nations under heaven."

Deuteronomy 4:19 NIV

"We need to find God, and he cannot be found in noise and restlessness. God is the friend of silence. See how nature—trees, flowers, grass—grows in silence; see the stars, the moon and the sun, how they move in silence... We need silence to be able to touch souls."

Mother Teresa,
Founder of the Missionaries of Charity
(1910–1997)

THE NORTH STAR will not always be the north star.

In fact "North Star" is only a nickname for Polaris, the brightest star in the constellation Ursa Minor. Yet even the name Polaris, which alludes to its status as the Earth's pole star, will be irrelevant in time. Due to the precession of the globe's axis (like the wobble of a spinning top), the North Pole will move away from Polaris beginning in the year 2100. At that point we might have to revert back to its less impressive name, "Alpha Ursae Minoris." But there is plenty of time before that happens. Vega will not take over as the new pole star until the year 14,000.

In addition to its status as pole star, Polaris is also a Cepheid variable star. Cepheids are unstable stars that change in apparent magnitude rather quickly (usually within a few days). These stars aid astronomers in calculating the distance of other galaxies. Polaris, at 400 light years away, pulses over an interval of about four days.

These two roles make Polaris one of the most familiar stars in the sky, despite the fact that it is only the 48th brightest. Yet there is one more reason why the North Star captures so much attention. Its constellation, Ursa Minor, is identifiable by even the most unaware stargazer as the "Little Dipper."

"God's promises are like the stars; the darker the night the brighter they shine."

David Nicholas

Polaris is quite an unusual star. First, Polaris is the nearest bright star to the north spin axis of the Earth. Therefore, as the Earth turns, stars appear to rotate around Polaris, making it the North Star. Since no bright star is near the south spin axis of the Earth, there is currently no South Star. WALLY PACHOLKA/ NASA/ GSFC

Gripped in the claw of the constellation Scorpius sits the reflection nebula DG 129, a cloud of gas and dust that reflects light from nearby, bright stars. NASA/JPL-CALTECH/UCLA

CHAPTER 6
THE MILKY WAY

"By faith we understand that the universe was formed at God's command, so that what is seen was not made out of what was visible."

Ephesians 4:7-10 CEV

Hundreds of thousands of stars crowd into the swirling core of our spiral Milky Way galaxy. The region pictured here is immense, with a horizontal span of 890 light-years and a vertical span of 640 light-years. Earth is located 26,000 light-years away, out in one of the Milky Way's spiral arms. NASA/JPL-CALTECH

SUN

Beyond Our Cosmic Neighborhood

WE HAVE NOW VISITED the moon, the sun, and the planets within our local solar system. It's time to move on and travel way beyond. Ahead of us is a universe so breathtakingly vast that only our imagination can explore its borders. Within our Milky Way alone, there are estimated to be 300 billion stars. If we counted one star a second, day and night, it would take over 9,512,937 years to count them all. And this is just in our own galaxy.

Until the beginning of the 20th century, it was believed that the Milky Way was the entirety of the universe, but a paper published by Edwin Hubble in 1925 asserted that the Milky Way is actually one of millions of similar galaxies throughout the universe.

Since Hubble's discoveries, we have learned much. As scientists look deeper and deeper into the universe, they see more and more galaxies without end. Current estimates are that there are from 250 billion to a trillion galaxies, each one having from 100 billion to a trillion stars or more.

"Then the LORD took Abram outside and said, 'Look at the sky and see if you can count the stars.'"

Genesis 15:5a CEV

"Somewhere, something incredible is waiting to be known."

Carl Sagan, American astronomer and cosmologist (1934–1996)

This image shows our own back yard, astronomically speaking, from a vantage point about 30 light-years away from the sun. It highlights the population of tiny brown dwarfs recently discovered by NASA's Wide-field Infrared Survey Explorer, or WISE (red circles). The image simulates actual positions of stars.

While big stars like our sun are flashy and easy to see from a distance, astronomers are also interested in our very faintest, smallest neighbors as well. One of the prime objectives of the WISE mission is to find missing "failed stars," or brown dwarfs, in the vicinity of the sun.

This rendering accurately portrays the relative positions of the sun and its surroundings as they would appear from a vantage point about 30 light-years away. The sun is the faint yellow dot at the very center.

NASA/JPL-CALTECH

Milky Way Basics

"There is for me powerful evidence that there is something going on behind it all... It seems as though somebody has fine-tuned nature's numbers to make the universe... The impression of design is overwhelming."

Paul Davies,
British theoretical physicist (1946–)

"Everything was created by him, everything in heaven and on earth, everything seen and unseen, including all forces and powers, and all rulers and authorities. All things were created by God's Son, and everything was made for him."

Colossians 1:16 CEV

A new, colorful collection of galaxy specimens showcases galaxies of several types, from elegant grand design spirals to more patchy flocculent spirals. Some of the galaxies have roundish centers, while others have elongated central bars. The orientation of the galaxies varies as well, with some seeming to peer straight back at us in the face-on configuration while others point to the side, appearing edge-on. Infrared light has been translated into colors we see with our eyes, such that the shortest wavelengths are blue and the longest are red. The oldest stars appear blue, while pockets of newly formed stars have yellow or reddish hues. (Facing page) This image of a pair of colliding galaxies called NGC 6240 shows them in a rare, short-lived phase of their evolution just before they merge into a single, larger galaxy. NASA/JPL-CALTECH/UCLA/STSCI-ESA

DESPITE BEING OUR EXTENDED "neighborhood," the Milky Way is hundreds of thousands of light years in diameter and thousands of light years thick. Designated as a spiral galaxy, the Milky Way is a vast and incredibly complex part of the universe; its scale is hard to imagine. The Milky Way is estimated to be made up of more than 200 billion stars, including the sun, and has an estimated mass of 400 billion solar masses. Because one solar mass is equivalent to the mass of the sun, then the entirety of the Milky Way is 400 billion times more massive.

Even if creation stopped at the limits of the Milky Way, there would exist enough of outer space for mankind to explore and wonder at forever.

The Local Group

"God lives in the heavens above the highest stars, where he sees everything. Do you think the deep darkness hides you from God?"

Job 22:12-13 CEV

One of our closest galactic neighbors shows its awesome beauty. M33, also known as the Triangulum Galaxy, is a member of what's known as our Local Group of galaxies. (Facing page) Sending chills down the spine of all arachnophobes is the Tarantula nebula, the largest star-forming region known in our entire Local Group of galaxies. NASA/JPL-CALTECH/UCLA

ASTRONOMERS BELIEVE that the universe could consist of up to one trillion galaxies, some of which include over one trillion stars. Our home galaxy is part of a.galaxy cluster called the Local Group, which is made up of about 30 to 40 other galaxies and is about 10 million light years across. The Milky Way is the second largest galaxy in the Local Group, and it is one of only three spiral galaxies. The rest are irregular or elliptical types. While studying the shapes and dynamics of other galaxies, Hubble found that they were actually moving away from the Milky Way. The conclusion that Hubble came to (now known as Hubble's Law) and which has become almost universally accepted, is that all galaxies are moving away from each other. The implication then is that, over time, the universe is thought to be expanding. Does this also imply that the galaxies originated from the same center?

Exactly how much, how fast, and for how long the universe could expand is not known, but for the time being the Milky Way and the Local Group of galaxies are drifting apart from each other – as the story of the galaxies continues to unfold.

"The significance and joy in my science comes in those occasional moments of discovering something new and saying to myself, 'So that's how God did it.' My goal is to understand a little corner of God's plan."

Henry "Fritz" Schaefer,
American theoretical chemist
(1944–)

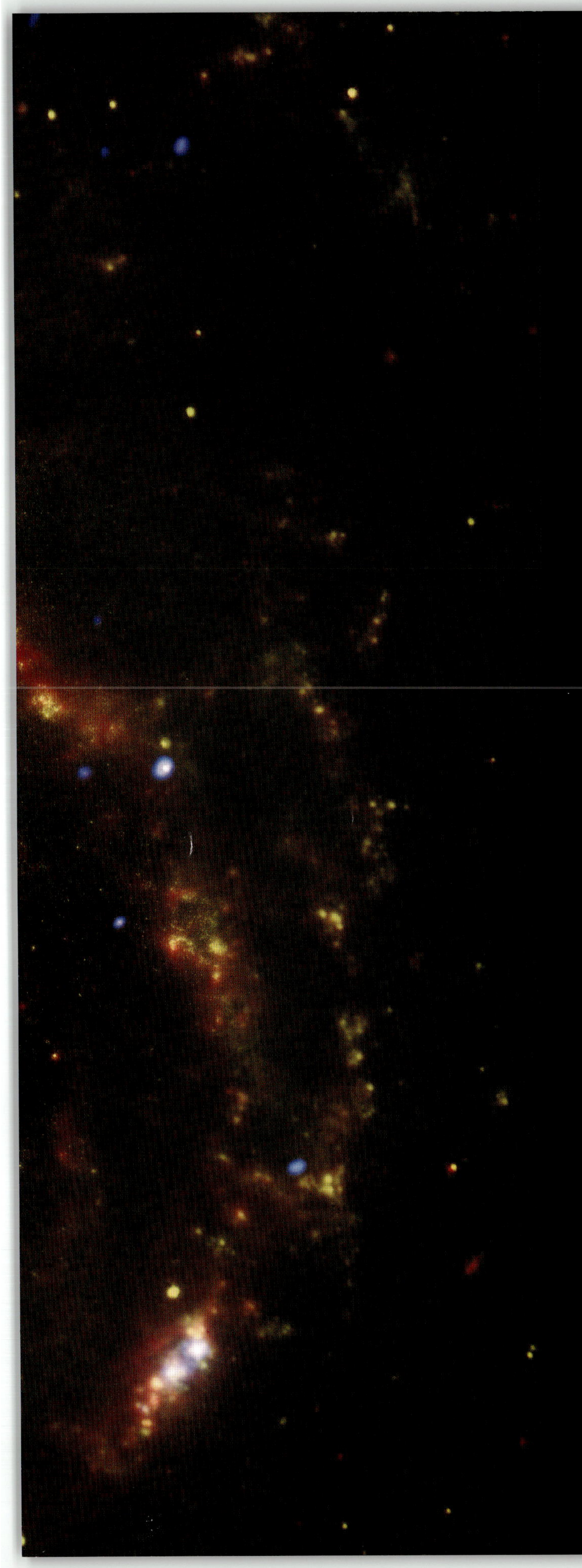

A Clearer Vision

OBSERVING THE MILKY WAY is like trying to look at your own nose without a mirror; if you look hard enough you can see part of it, but you never get the whole picture.

Much of our previous understanding of the universe is changing. The belief that the solar system lies near the center of the Milky Way, as was long believed, is simply wrong.

Recent calculations place the sun about halfway between the core and the outer edge of the galaxy. This also affects the relative location of the Earth in the Milky Way, which, it turns out, is a good thing.

Another advantage to being farther from the center than originally thought is that the galaxy is more observable. When Earth faces Sagittarius (the center of the Milky Way), we can get a relatively broad view of the galaxy – a view that looks like a trail of spilled milk in the sky.

"If the ratio of the nuclear strong force to the electromagnetic force had been different by 1 part in 1016, no stars could have formed. Again, the ratio of the electromagnetic force-constant to the gravitational force-constant must be equally delicately balanced. Increase it by only 1 part in 1040 and only small stars can exist; decrease it by the same amount and there will only be large stars. You must have both large and small stars in the universe: the large ones produce elements in their thermonuclear furnaces; and it is only the small ones that burn long enough to sustain a planet with life… The impression of design is overwhelming."

Paul Davies, British theoretical physicist (1946–)

"For great is your love, higher than the heavens; your faithfulness reaches to the skies."

Psalm 108:4 NIV

NASA's Great Observatories are continuing Galileo's legacy with stunning images and breakthrough science from the Hubble Space Telescope, the Spitzer Space Telescope, and the Chandra X-ray Observatory.

While Galileo observed the sky using visible light seen by the human eye, technology now allows us to observe in many wavelengths, including Spitzer's infrared view and Chandra's view in X-rays. Each wavelength region shows different aspects of celestial objects and often reveals new objects that could not otherwise be studied.

This image of the spiral galaxy Messier 101 is a composite of views from Spitzer, Hubble, and Chandra.

Such composite images allow astronomers to see how features seen in one wavelength match up with those seen in another wavelength. It's like seeing with a camera, night vision goggles, and X-ray vision all at once. NASA/ESA/CXC/SSC/STSCI

The Hole in the Middle

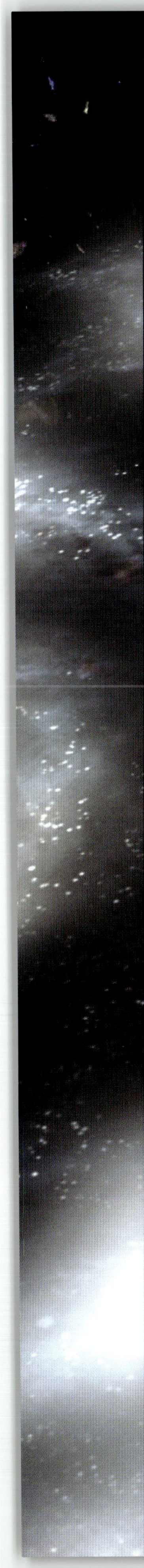

"In the fall of 1967, [I was invited] to a conference... on pulsars.... In my talk, I argued that we should consider the possibility that the center of a pulsar is a gravitationally completely collapsed object. I remarked that one couldn't keep saying 'gravitationally completely collapsed object' over and over. One needed a shorter descriptive phrase. 'How about black hole?' asked someone in the audience. I had been searching for the right term for months, mulling it over in bed, in the bathtub, in my car, whenever I had quiet moments. Suddenly this name seemed exactly right."

John Wheeler,
American physicist
(1911–2008)

AT THE CENTER of the Milky Way there exists a mysterious and fascinating phenomenon known as a black hole where the gravitational field is so powerful that even light cannot escape its pull. Black holes are massive areas of spacetime that may be the gravitational result of a collapsing star at the end of its life cycle. Despite the difficulty presented in studying these distant cosmic "holes" which emit and reflect no light, it is believed that black holes exist at the center of most if not all galaxies.

Scientists believe the black hole at the center of the Milky Way is ten times the physical size of the sun and has a mass of approximately four million times that of the sun. This supermassive black hole is called Sagittarius A* (pronounced Sagittarius A star), and it lies 26,000 light years away from Earth nestled in the center of the galaxy, a source of great fascination and intrigue for astronomers and stargazers alike.

Though many theories exist about the nature of black holes, much is still currently not known today about their exact dynamics. How did they come to be? Do they have a life span? And, most interestingly of all, if something were to pass through the unimaginable power of a black hole, where would it go?

"If I go up to the heavens, you are there; if I make my bed in the depths, you are there. If I rise on the wings of the dawn, if I settle on the far side of the sea, even there your hand will guide me, your right hand will hold me fast."

Psalm 139:7-8 NIV

This artist's concept shows a galaxy with a supermassive black hole at its core. Black holes are immense distortions of space and time with gravity that is so great, even light itself cannot escape. NASA/JPL-CALTECH

Hypervelocity Planets

WHILE SOME PLANETS in the Milky Way float freely around at their own rate and speed, others are hurtled through space by hyper intensive energy. These planets are sometimes even flung out of the galaxy. Astronomers believe these "hypervelocity planets" are traveling through the galaxy at up to almost 50 million km/h (31 million miles/hour). In 2005 scientists discovered the first hypervelocity star, which is flying toward the edge of the galaxy at 2.4 million km/h (1.4 million miles/hour).

These hypervelocity bodies are expelled from the galaxy and the galaxy's gravitational pull by what amounts to gravitational "slingshots." If you imagine a child's slingshot used to propel small rocks through the air but replace the small rock with a massive planet or star and then replace the slingshot with the unlimited force of gravity-breaking energy, you get hypervelocity. Just another of our galaxy's displays of power, speed, and exceptional force.

"The greatest discoveries of science have always been those that forced us to rethink our beliefs about the universe and our place in it."

Robert L. Park,
professor of physics (1931–)

"I praise you forever, Lord! … Your power is great, and your glory is seen everywhere in heaven and on earth. You are king of the entire world, and you rule with strength and power."

1 Chronicles 29:10-12 CEV

A hundred million years ago, a triple-star system was traveling through the bustling center of our Milky Way galaxy when it made a life-changing misstep. The trio wandered too close to the galaxy's giant black hole, which captured one of the stars and hurled the other two out of the Milky Way. Adding to the stellar game of musical chairs, the two outbound stars merged to form a super- hot, blue star. NASA, ESA, AND G. BACON (STSCI)

The Aging Galaxy

THE PROCESS OF VISIBLE aging is not just confined to us humans. Much like how human aging becomes apparent in the loss or graying of hair, aging galaxies also experience a change in appearance. When a galaxy is young, it appears to be blue because it contains the most short-lived massive and hot stars. Older galaxies on the other end of the age and color spectrum appear red because they have seized forming stars long ago, and all the short-lived massive and hot stars have died. The Milky Way, however, is in its "middle age," meaning it is transitioning into a more dormant and "red" stage of existence.

The aging of the Milky Way reminds us that all parts of the universe are changing, evolving, aging – the process of time marches forward always turning something into something else.

"Other nations worship idols, but the Lord created the heavens. Give honor and praise to the Lord, whose power and beauty fill his holy temple."

1 Chronicles 16:26-27 CEV

"Astronomy compels the soul to look upwards and leads us from this world to another."

Plato, Greek philosopher (427 - 347 BC)

Our Consumer Galaxy

OPTICAL IMAGE OF THE MILKY WAY GALAXY BY E. SLAWIK

CHANDRA X-RAY IMAGE OF SAGITTARIUS A*

"Everything in the heavens has a body, and so does everything on earth. But each one is very different from all the others. The sun isn't like the moon, the moon isn't like the stars, and each star is different."
1 Corinthians 15:40-41 CEV

WHILE THE BLACK HOLE at the center of our galaxy is relatively dormant now, faint gamma ray bubbles seen recently by the Fermi telescope give the impression that Sagittarius A* (or Sgr A*) was once a very active black hole. Whenever Sgr A* consumes smaller space debris, it emits faint bursts of radiation. But when Fermi identified two visible gamma ray bubbles measuring 27,000 light years across (evidence of a much greater explosion or consumption), astronomers believed that something bigger had once occurred. It is now believed that these immense gamma ray jets are an after-image of a major consumption that occurred in the Milky Way's distant past. Perhaps the Milky Way, via its black center, absorbed a system of planets, a star, or a gas cloud.

Astronomers have long known that the supermassive black hole at the center of the Milky Way Galaxy, known as Sagittarius A (or Sgr A* for short), is a particularly poor eater. The fuel for this black hole comes from powerful winds blown off dozens of massive young stars that are concentrated nearby. These stars are located a relatively large distance away from Sgr A*, where the gravity of the black hole is weak, and so their high-velocity winds are difficult for the black hole to capture and swallow. Scientists have previously calculated that Sgr A* should consume only about 1% of the fuel carried in the winds.* NASA/CXC/MIT/F.K. BAGANOFF ET AL.

"Nature is an infinite sphere whereof the centre is everywhere, the circumference nowhere. In short, imagination is brought to silence at the thought, and that is the most perceptible sign of the all-power of God." Blaise Pascal, French mathematician and physicist (1623–1662)

CHAPTER 7

OTHER GALAXIES

"Bless the Lord, O my soul! O Lord my God, you are very great! You are clothed with splendor and majesty, covering yourself with light as with a garment, stretching out the heavens like a tent." Psalm 104:1-2 ESV

A "landscape" image from the cosmos. Cutting across a nearby star-forming region are the "hills and valleys" of gas and dust displayed in intricate detail. Set amid a backdrop of soft, glowing blue light are wispy tendrils of gas as well as dark trunks of dust that are light-years in height. NASA, ESA, AND THE HUBBLE HERITAGE TEAM (STSCI/AURA)

Serenity in Motion

IT IS COMMONLY KNOWN that Earth spins on an axis. This is why the sun appears to rise and set. And while the Earth spins on its axis, it also revolves around the sun, giving the planet seasons because of the tilt of the globe. Zooming out, the Local Group of galaxies itself, which includes the Milky Way, is traveling towards a cluster of galaxies called the Virgo Supercluster.

Add Earth's spin around its axis (1000 km/h) (621 miles/h) to Earth's rotation around the Sun (100,000 km/h) (62,137 miles/hour) to the solar system's flight into the Milky Way (close to one million km/h) (621,371 miles/hour) to the Milky Way's speed through space towards distant galaxies (over two million km/h) (1,2 million miles/hour), and you get an idea of what an incredible space flight you are on. Added all up, your speed amounts to roughly 3.1 million km/h (1.9 million miles/hour)!

Yet, back on Earth you can lie in your bed or sit upon a beach listening to the sounds of the waves and be completely oblivious to the cosmic enormity in it all. We are part of a grand story – which spins and turns fantastically all around us.

"From down here on earth, everyone has looked up and seen how great God is – God is more than we imagine; no one can count the years he has lived."

Job 36:25-26 CEV

"The most incomprehensible thing about the universe is that it is comprehensible."

Albert Einstein,
Swiss theoretical physicist
(1879–1955)

This composite image shows a supernova within the galaxy M100 that may contain the youngest known black hole in our cosmic neighborhood. The galaxy M100 is located in the Virgo Cluster about 50 million light-years from Earth. NASA/JPL/CALTECH

Untold Galaxies

IT IS IRONIC that the more human technology advances allowing us to peer deeper and deeper into space, the more we become aware of just how small we are. Estimates based on data from Hubble observations reveal that the Milky Way is only one of billions of observable galaxies. This is a humbling revelation.

Although most galaxies are irregularly shaped, many take the distinctive form of either a spiral or an ellipsis.

"Every good and perfect gift comes down from the Father who created all the lights in the heavens. He is always the same and never makes dark shadows by changing."

James 1:17 CEV

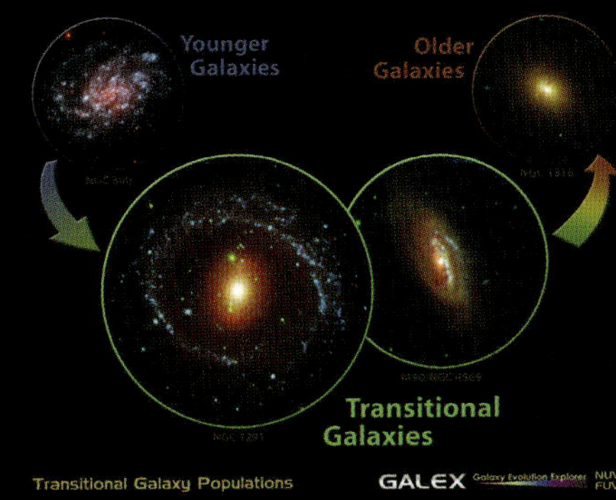

New evidence from NASA's Galaxy Evolution Explorer supports the long-held notion that many galaxies begin life as smaller spirals before transforming into larger, elliptical-shaped galaxies. Examples of young, teenage and adult galaxies are shown here from left to right. NASA/JPL-CALTECH/CTIO/LAS CAMPANAS/PALOMAR

Spirals are what most picture when they think about a galaxy – with tentacle-like arms wrapped around the core in a flattened disc-like shape. This familiarity is due in part because our own galaxy, the Milky Way, is a spiral and also because, visually, spirals are the most interesting. In addition to their fascinating shape, they also feature multiple generations of stars, giving the galaxies a variety of color.

Ellipticals are ovoid in shape and often uniform in color, a yellowish glow from an older collection of stars. They are generally short on gas and dust, the star-creating material, thus new star formation in this type of galaxy is rare.

Just how many galaxies are in the universe is not known, but there are likely many other galaxy shapes, types, and phenomena to be discovered as we continue our exploration of the universe. The myriads of galaxies we can see might very well be a minute atomic structure of a much larger body of galaxies, which again might be the atomic structure of some even larger entity.

"Aiming at the stars, both literally and figuratively, is the work of generations, but no matter how much progress one makes there is always the thrill of just beginning."

Robert Goddard, American physicist (1882–1945)

The central region of our Milky Way galaxy. In this spectacular image, observations using infrared light and X-ray light see through the obscuring dust and reveal the intense activity near the galactic core. Note that the center of the galaxy is located within the bright white region to the right of and just below the middle of the image. NASA/JPL-CALTECH/ESA/CXC/STSCI

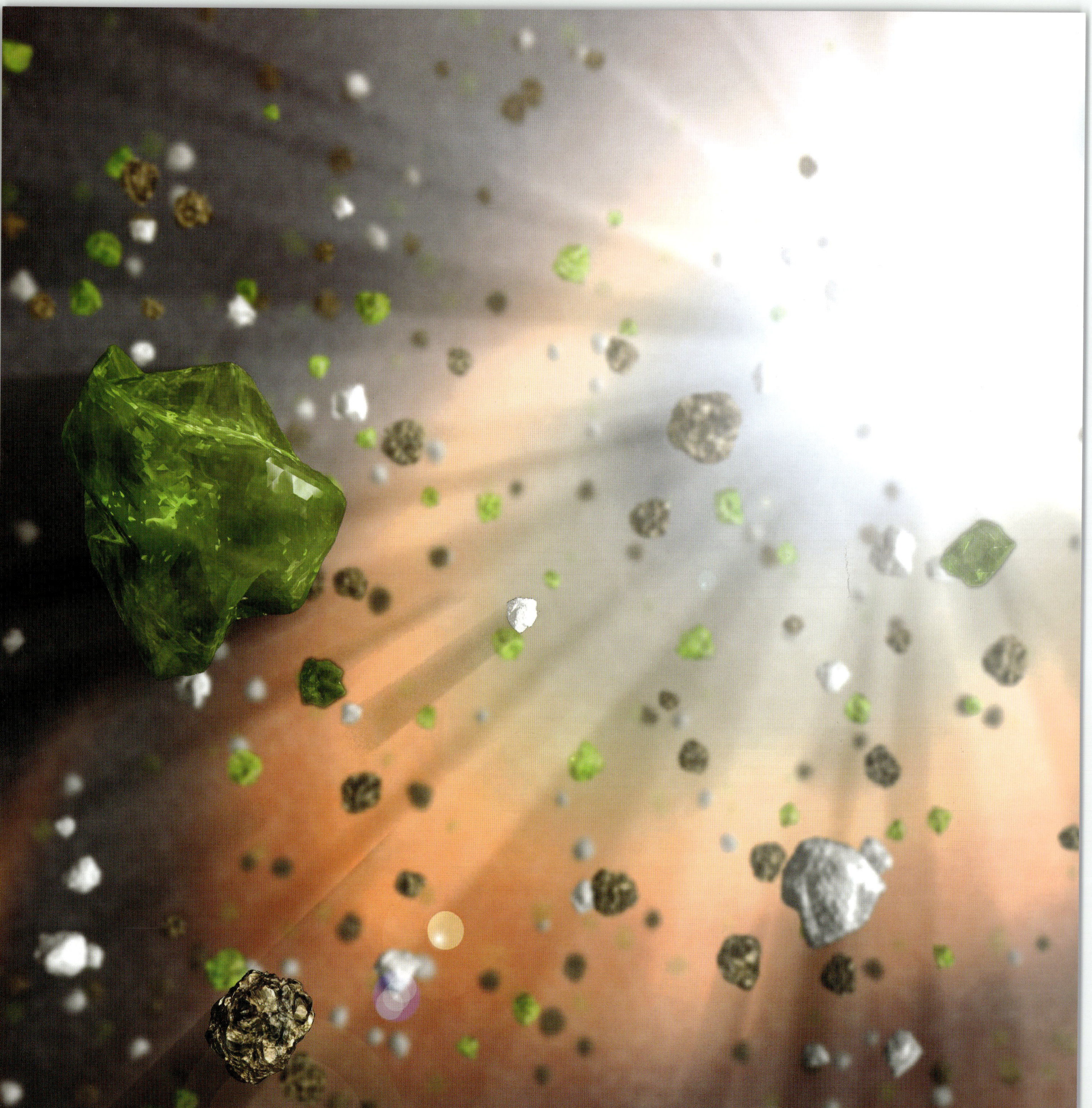

More Than Stars

Galaxy with an Active Galactic Nucleus

Quasar

"The universe is simple; it's the explanation that's complex."

Anonymous

WHEN VIEWED FROM our earthly vantage point, quasars look much like stars. Even the word "quasar" comes from "quasi-stellar" because of the visual similarity. But, in fact, quasars are much more brilliant than stars. The only reason they bear resemblance at all is that they are so far away – thought to be billions of light years away – that their light source is diminished to the level of stellar objects.

In actuality, a quasar is an active galactic nucleus powered by a supermassive black hole, hungrily consuming all surrounding material including stars. The pull of a quasar's black hole creates a spinning doughnut of debris around it called an accretion disc. The matter that escapes the black hole – which is not much – is shot out perpendicularly on either side of the doughnut creating a line straight through the middle. The accretion disc spins at such a rapid rate that the matter inside becomes hot and glows.

To put things in perspective, though quasars are generally not much larger than our own solar system, they can have a mass over 1 billion times greater. In addition, the most impressive quasars emit 10 million times more radio energy than the Milky Way and 100 times more light, making them brighter than all the stars of their galaxy combined.

"I praise you, Lord God, with all my heart. You are glorious and majestic, dressed in royal robes and surrounded by light." Psalm 104:1-2a CEV

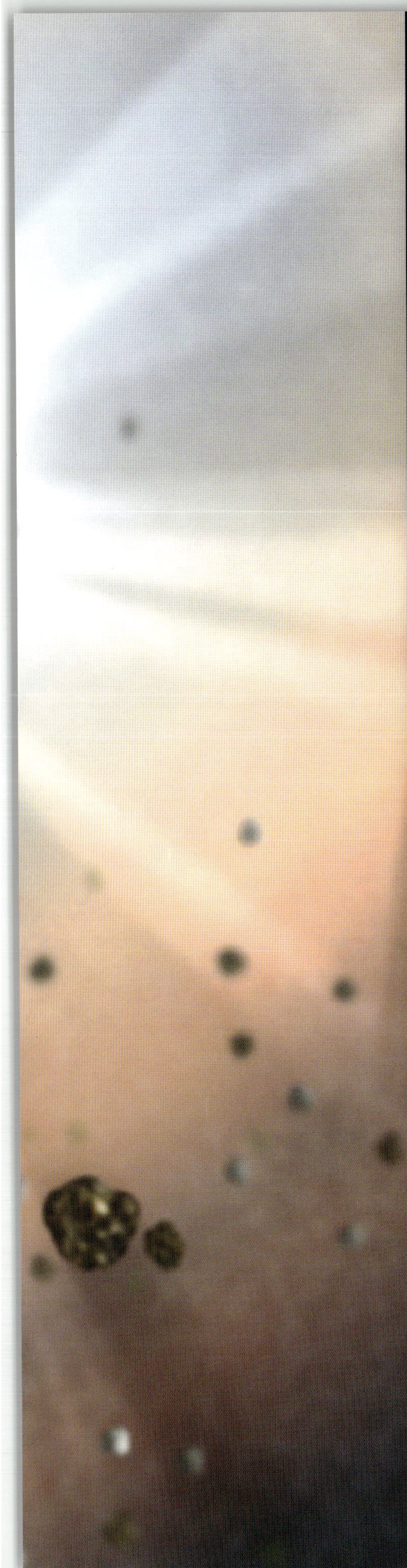

Dusty grains—including tiny specks of the minerals found in the gemstones peridot, sapphires and rubies—can be seen blowing in the winds of a quasar, or active black hole, in this artist's concept. NASA/JPL-CALTECH

Our Heavenly Neighbor

LOOKING INTO THE COSMOS, thousands of densely-packed specks of light illuminate an otherwise black background. Upon closer examination, several large spirals spin in the distance. Many more ellipticals fill the canvas and give off a whitish glow. This is the Virgo Group. Also known as the Virgo Cluster, it is 15 million light years in diameter. But as large as the Virgo Group is, it is only a part of an even bigger structure.

The Virgo Supercluster is a collection of smaller clusters of galaxies including the Local Group (containing our own Milky Way) and the Virgo Group. That the group shares its name with its supercluster is no coincidence at all. The Virgo Group is so massive that it is the center and anchor of the supercluster. Due to the extreme gravitational pull of the Virgo Group, the Local Group is moving towards it at a rate of 1.4 million km/h (869,920 miles/hour).

Part of Virgo's density is due to the presence of M87, one of the universe's most massive elliptical galaxies. Another contributing factor is that though the Virgo Group is only fifty percent larger (by diameter) than the Local Group, it has about 400 times more galaxies jammed into that space.

Virgo is our nearest galaxy cluster neighbor at a distance of about 47 million light years. Yet despite this long distance, some of the galaxies belonging to Virgo are bright enough that even with limited available instruments, astronomers 200 years ago could see them.

"Lord God All-Powerful of Israel, your throne is above the winged creatures. You created the heavens and the earth, and you alone rule the kingdoms of this world."

Isaiah 37:16 CEV

"The discovery of one star is the promise of another."

Robert Aris Willmott, British poet (1809–1863)

Arp 274, also known as NGC 5679, is a system of three galaxies that appear to be partially overlapping in the image, although they may be at somewhat different distances. The entire system resides at about 400 million light-years away from Earth in the constellation Virgo. NASA, ESA, AND M. LIVIO AND THE HUBBLE HERITAGE TEAM (STSCI/AURA)

Two Galaxies in One

THE GALAXY CENTAURUS A is not directly named after the fictitious centaur. The name actually comes from the galaxy's host constellation, simply called Centaurus. Yet, just like the centaur, NGC5128 is actually two creatures merged into one. But instead of a horse and a man, it is a combined elliptical and a spiral galaxy.

Centaurus A's form results from a great galactic collision. Two galaxies, an elliptical and a spiral, collided and merged to form a new galaxy. The elliptical because it was more massive most likely attracted the spiral by its gravitational pull and then cannibalized it. The merger spurred new star formation, creating an interesting mixture of young stars with the older stars already in existence within the elliptical. Another result of the merger is a supermassive black hole 250 times larger than that of the Milky Way.

Centaurus A, the vibrant hybrid, is the brightest galaxy outside of the Local Group and the fifth known brightest galaxy overall.

"He decided how many stars there would be in the sky and gave each one a name. Our Lord is great and powerful! He understands everything."

Psalm 147:4-5 CEV

"Why it is that of all the billions and billions of strange objects in the Cosmos—novas, quasars, pulsars, black holes—you are beyond doubt the strangest?"

Walker Percy, American novelist (1916–1990)

This image of Centaurus A shows a spectacular new view of a supermassive black hole's power. . The x-ray jet in the upper left extends for about 13,000 light years away from the black hole. The APEX data shows that material in the jet is traveling at about half the speed of light.
NASA/CXC/CFA/R.KRAFT ET AL.

Quality Over Quantity

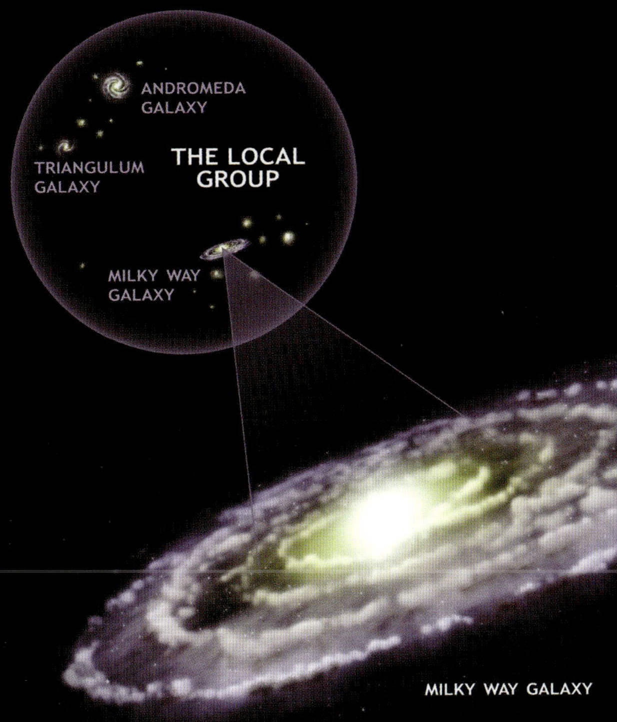

"Two things fill the mind with ever new and increasing admiration and awe, the oftener and more steadily they are reflected on: the starry heavens above me and the moral law within me."

Immanuel Kant, German philosopher (1724–1804)

JUDGING BY QUANTITY, the cluster of galaxies known as the Local Group is probably not worth mentioning. It has only an estimated 40 galaxies – a small amount compared with its neighbor the Virgo Group which has more than 2,000. But looking beyond the numbers reveals some of the most interesting galaxies in the known universe.

While most galaxy clusters are dominated by ellipticals and indeed even the majority of galaxies in the Local Group are dwarf ellipticals as well, it is the awesomeness of the Local Group's three spiral galaxies that makes it special. While ellipticals generally appear homogeneous and monochrome, the Local Group's spirals excite the imagination with their variations in hue and shape thanks to those octopus-like tentacles.

The other two spirals joining the Milky Way are Triangulum and Andromeda. These galaxies combined with the Small and Large Magellanic Clouds make a total of five galaxies visible from Earth with the naked eye.

Hence the name "Local Group" – not flashy, but informative. That the Milky Way and our neighboring galaxies are part of a group is not remarkable; isolated galaxies are a rarity in the universe. In fact, the majority of Local Group's galaxies are actually satellites around the cluster's two main members, the Milky Way and Andromeda. Without those two, there would be no Local Group.

"Jesus said, 'Did I not tell you that if you believed you would see the glory of God?'"

John 11:40 ESV

The immense Andromeda galaxy is the closest large galaxy to our Milky Way galaxy, and is located 2.5 million light-years from our sun. It is close enough for telescopes to spy the details of its ringed arms of new stars and hazy blue backbone of older stars. The Andromeda galaxy is larger than our Milky Way and contains more stars, but the Milky Way is thought to perhaps have more mass due to its larger proportion of a mysterious substance called dark matter. Both galaxies belong to our so-called Local Group, a collection of more than 50 galaxies, most of which are tiny dwarf systems.
NASA/JPL-CALTECH/UCLA

A Galaxy of Many Names

"It is unlikely that we will ever see a star being born. Stars are like animals in the wild. We may see the very young, but never their actual birth, which is a veiled and secret event. Stars are born inside thick clouds of dust and gas in the spiral arms of the galaxy, so thick that visible light cannot penetrate them."

Heinz R. Pagels, American physicist (1939–1988)

THE TRIANGULUM GALAXY has many aliases. It is known by no less than four names: Triangulum – because it lies within the eponymous constellation, M33, NGC 598, and The Pinwheel Galaxy. But do not confuse this galaxy with M101 that shares the nickname Pinwheel. M101 is ten times farther away. The galactic arms of this spiral galaxy indicate apparent motion like a pinwheel begging to be blown, and it is nearly as colorful with pinks, yellows, and blues throughout.

Although Triangulum is the third largest galaxy in the Local Group, it is relatively small at 50,000 light years in diameter. By comparison, Andromeda is 140,000 light years across, and in fact Triangulum is one of Andromeda's many satellite galaxies. As a member of the Local Cluster, the galaxy lies 2.7 million light years away. Yet because it faces Earth, it is spread out over a wider spectrum making it faint in the sky. When visible, it appears twice the size of the full moon.

But although it is faint, one of the most notable features is NGC 604, a large star-forming nebula at the edge of the galaxy that appears bright red. In fact, star formation is what Triangulum does best. Scattered throughout the galaxy are pink dots which indicate gas conducive to star creation. So although it is faint and small, Triangulum can boast that it has a higher rate of star formation than either the Milky Way or Andromeda.

"The holy God asks, 'Who compares with me? Is anyone my equal?' Look at the evening sky! Who created the stars? Who gave them each a name? Who leads them like an army? The Lord is so powerful that none of the stars are ever missing."

Isaiah 40:25-26 CEV

The Triangulum Galaxy is located nearly 3 million light years from Earth. And, in a study that pushes the limits of observations currently possible from Earth, a team of NASA and European scientists recorded the "fingerprints" of mystery molecules in the Triangulum Galaxy, as well as the Andromeda Galaxy. NASA/SWIFT SCIENCE TEAM/STEFAN IMMLER

A Glimpse Into the Distance

THE ANDROMEDA GALAXY is so bright that even though it is 2.5 million light years from Earth, it can be seen with the naked eye.

In fact Andromeda, also known as M31, has the distinction of being the most distant object visible from Earth without the use of instruments. To understand just how incredible it is that a human standing on Earth can see even a portion of Andromeda, consider this: one light year is approximately 9.46 trillion kilometers (5.86 trillion miles). Multiply that by 2.5 million, and that is how far away Andromeda is – a number basically incomprehensible to us.

"The universe begins to look more like a great thought than a machine." Sir James Jeans, British physicist (1877–1946)

"How great is God's love for all who worship him? Greater than the distance between heaven and earth! How far has the Lord taken our sins from us? Farther than the distance from east to west!"

Psalm 103:11-12 CEV

Another perspective on such a distance is this: the Andromeda Galaxy is one of the few that is actually moving towards our own Milky Way rather than away from it. The two galaxies are moving towards one another at an astonishing rate of 120 km/s (75 m/s). Yet even at this breakneck speed, it will still take around 5 billion years for the two to collide, or about 5.2 million life spans of Methuselah, the oldest man recorded in history at 969 years old (Genesis 5:27).

The immense Andromeda galaxy is the closest large galaxy to our Milky Way galaxy, and is located 2.5 million light-years from our sun. It is close enough for telescopes to spy the details of its ringed arms of new stars and hazy blue backbone of older stars. The Andromeda galaxy is larger than our Milky Way and contains more stars, but the Milky Way is thought to perhaps have more mass due to its larger proportion of a mysterious substance called dark matter. Both galaxies belong to our so-called Local Group, a collection of more than 50 galaxies, most of which are tiny dwarf systems.

NASA/JPL-CALTECH/UCLA

Magellan's Clouds

ALTHOUGH FERDINAND MAGELLAN died during his attempt to circumnavigate the globe in the early sixteenth century, he was fortunate enough to observe something mostly unknown to the rest of the northern world. In the midst of sailing the southern latitudes, he observed two galaxies that now bear his name: *The Large and Small Magellanic Clouds.*

These terms "small" and "large" are used in reference to one another – the Large Magellanic Cloud (LMC) is ten times larger than the Small (SMC). But these adjectives exemplify the nature of relativity. At a mass of around 7 billion suns, the Small Magellanic Cloud (SMC) should perhaps more appropriately be named the Smaller Yet Still Massive Magellanic Cloud (SUSMMC). And the LMC, despite its name, is 1/20 the size of the Milky Way by diameter.

The LMC and SMC are two of the galaxies closest to our own at 160,000 and 200,000 light years away respectively. Because of this proximity, the Magellanic Clouds were once thought to be satellite galaxies of the Milky Way. But recent calculations estimate that they are travelling at 500 km/s (300 m/s) (984 feet/s) – too quickly to be in orbit around us.

At that speed Magellan could have traversed the entire planet in less than three minute's time. Of course, while lying on the deck of his ship and staring up at the stars, this movement was imperceptible – a testament to the extreme distance of these "close" galaxies. Instead, what he saw amidst a field of millions of stars were two gaseous "clouds" that have since been found to be much more than just clouds.

"He (Jesus) is the radiance of the glory of God and the exact imprint of his nature, and he upholds the universe by the word of his power. After making purification for sins, he sat down at the right hand of the Majesty on high."

Hebrews 1:3 ESV

"Those who study the stars have God for a teacher."

Tycho Brahe,
Danish astronomer
(1546–1601)

The Large Magellanic Cloud, located 160,000 light-years from Earth, is one of a handful of dwarf galaxies that orbit our own Milky Way. It is approximately one-third as wide as the Milky Way, and, if it could be seen in its entirety, would cover the same amount of sky as a grid of about 480 full moons. NASA/JPL-CALTECH/STSCI

CHAPTER 8

THE MYSTERIOUS UNIVERSE

"Astronomy leads us to a unique event, a universe which was created out of nothing, one with the very delicate balance needed to provide exactly the right conditions required to permit life, and one which has an underlying (one might say 'supernatural') plan."

Arno Penzias, Nobel Prize winner in physics (1933–)

"The Lord says: 'My thoughts and my ways are not like yours. Just as the heavens are higher than the earth, my thoughts and my ways are higher than yours.'"

Isaiah 55:8-9 CEV

The cloud, located about 6,000 light-years away in the constellation Sagittarius, is dominated by a central group of massive stars—the most massive stars in the region. These central stars give off intense flows of expanding gas, which rush like rivers against dense piles of material, carving out the deep pocket at center of the picture. Winds from the region's other massive stars push back against these oncoming rivers, creating bow shocks like those that pile up in front of speeding boats. NASA/JPL-CALTECH/UNIV. OF WISC.

'The All'

IN THE MOST GENERAL TERMS, the universe can be described as everything that exists, and that includes all that we can touch, observe, and imagine – even those things we do not and may never discover or comprehend. The universe is, quite literally, everything.

Though the English word "universe" comes from the Latin "unvorsum" which means everything rotated as one, the idea of a connected "universe" dates back further than Rome. What in modern terms could be called the universe, nature, or reality was known by the ancient Greeks as the "All." The Greek "All" was an idea of an absolute, though not necessarily personal, God – intelligent, beyond man's full understanding, creative, and fatherlike. Aristotle acknowledged that behind or within the "All", behind everything, there was a "prime mover" – an unmoved being that had set everything else in motion without itself being set in motion.

For the ancients, complexity and simplicity, vastness and intricacy, physics and metaphysics, natural laws and the phenomena of miracles (or violations to the natural laws) were not ideas broken into distinct scientific and theological fields. Throughout the ages the study of anything and the study of everything have both been attempts to understand the same universe, to understand the "All"... to understand God. In this way, since the beginning of time, the investigation of creation has always been a search for the Creator.

"For since the creation of the world God's invisible qualities—his eternal power and divine nature—have been clearly seen, being understood from what has been made, so that people are without excuse." Romans 1:20 NIV

"Quantum mechanics is certainly imposing. But an inner voice tells me that this is not yet the real thing. The theory says a lot, but does not bring us any closer to the secrets of the Old One. I, at any rate, am convinced that He is not playing at dice."

Albert Einstein,
Swiss theoretical physicist
(1879–1955)

"The heavens declare the glory of God; the skies proclaim the work of his hands. Day after day they pour forth speech; night after night they reveal knowledge."

Psalm 19:1-2 NIV

The "Pacman Nebula" is located about 9,200 light years from Earth and, remarkably, almost 1,000 light years above the plane of the Galaxy, giving astronomers a nearly unfettered view of the star formation within it. NASA/CXC/CFA/S.WOLK

The Limit of the Limitless

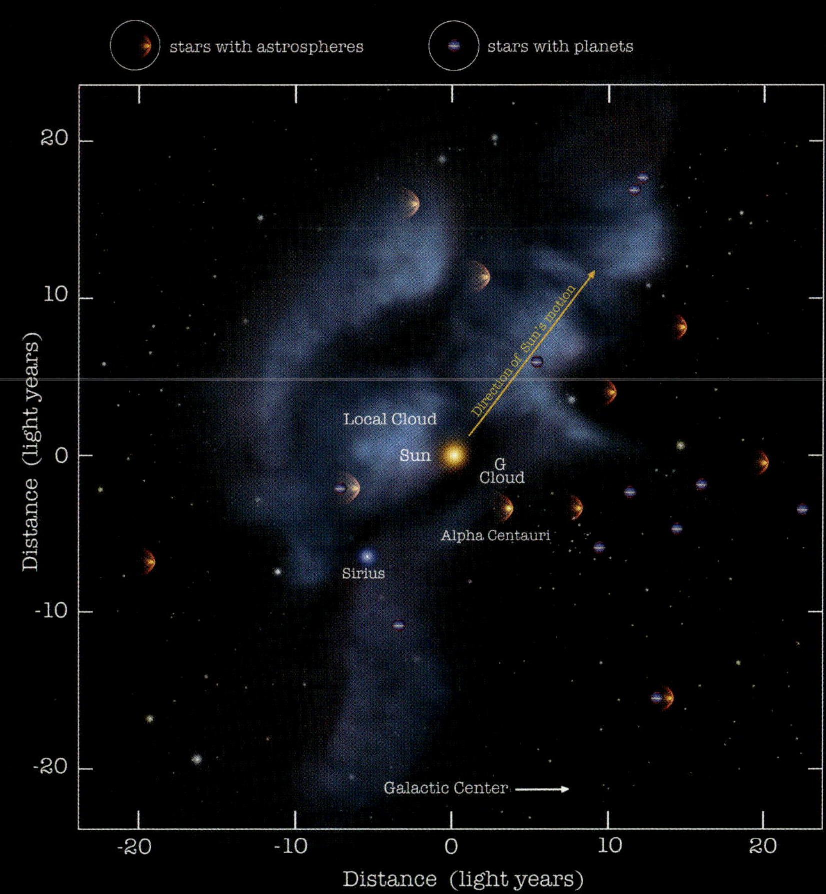

THE UNIVERSE IS BIG – unimaginably big – and, as such, the vast and infinitely complex nature of the universe requires its own field of astronomy known as cosmology. Though cosmology is the crossroads between the theoretical and scientific study of the origins, laws, and development of the seemingly limitless universe – cosmologists themselves are limited in one significant way – by how much of the universe they can actually see.

Within cosmology, there is a marked distinction between the universe in its entirety and the "observable universe" – which is limited to those things that theoretically could be visible on Earth (based on variant theories of the universe's age and therefore the distance light could travel during that time period). Though most astronomers believe that the universe is expanding, there is also an understanding that far beyond the limit of our vision there are light sources (such as stars) whose emission have yet to reach Earth and our telescopes. The further any object is from our solar system the longer it will take for its light to reach us. And so, an untold number of galaxies will remain in darkness until some time in the future when their light finally reaches us and our understanding of the universe expands along with our vision.

But for now, there is more than enough in the cosmos to explore – infinitely more.

"The Lord has kept the heavens for himself, but he has given the earth to us humans."

Psalm 115:16 CEV

"Astronomers work always with the past; because light takes time to move from one place to another, they see things as they were, not as they are."

Neale Eltinge Howard,
American science writer
(1911–)

The Rosette nebula, a turbulent star-forming region located 5,000 light-years away in the constellation Monoceros.
NASA/JPL-CALTECH/UNIV. OF ARIZ.

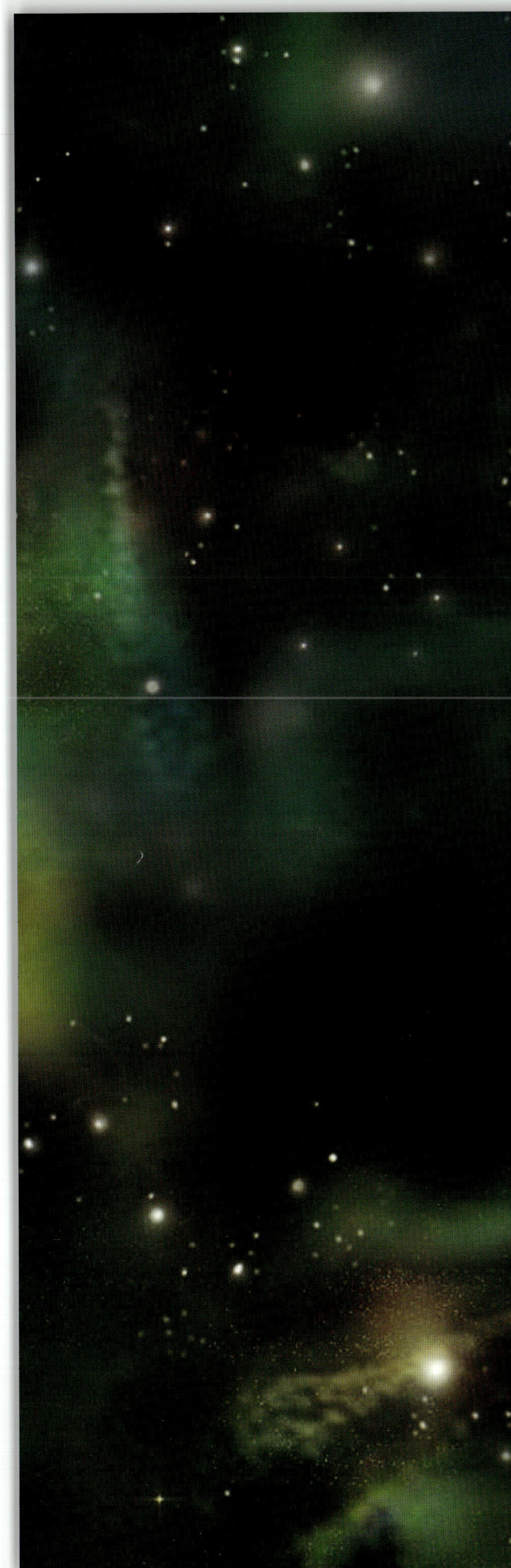

Origin and Expansion

AS ASTRONOMERS and physicists seek to understand the nature of the universe, three questions at the forefront of their field remain a mystery: how and when exactly did the universe begin, and how is it changing over time?

While variations on "Big Bang" cosmology are the leading theories on the origins of the universe, these are still theoretical and rely on hypothetical concepts based on mathematical models that extrapolate backwards from modern observations of galaxy movements. These models, based on the galactic observations of Edwin Hubble in the 1920s, suggest that the further away a galaxy is from Earth, the faster it is moving away from Earth. Therefore, it is deducted that the universe is continuously expanding. Since Hubble's studies, it has become widely accepted that the universe is expanding equally in all directions and that the universe is also curved. When scientists work backwards using this same theory, they deduce a fixed point in history, approximately 14 billion years ago, when they believe the universe as we know it was born.

While still the most widely accepted model in the scientific community, the "Big Bang" theory is not a complete explanation of the universe's origin, and many secular scientists are abandoning it. Eventhough this theory is more fiction than proven fact, it is the most developed scientific theory of the origin of the universe. And with each new discovery about the origin and expansion of the universe, a myriad of new questions is born. In many ways, the more that is revealed, the more we must confess that we do not know.

"I am the Lord God. I created the heavens like an open tent above. I made the earth and everything that grows on it. I am the source of life for all who live on this earth, so listen to what I say."

Isaiah 42:5 CEV

"If you thought that science was certain – well, that is just an error on your part."

Richard P. Feynman,
American theoretical physicist
(1918 - 1988)

Gamma-ray bursts are the universe's biggest explosions, capable of producing so much light that ground-based telescopes easily detect it billions of light-years away. In this artist's concept, dense knots of dust in otherwise normal galaxies dim the light of a dark gamma-ray burst (center). NASA/SWIFT/ AURORE SIMONNET

Dark Energy

"The universe is full of magical things patiently waiting for our wits to grow sharper."

Eden Phillpotts, British poet, from "A Shadow Passes" (1862–1960)

NOT ONLY DOES the universe expand, it expands with an ever faster speed. If gravity is always pulling things inward acting in opposition to expansion or outward drift, then how can the whole of the universe be expanding with accelerating speed?

If we assume the universal expansion is accelerating based on the findings of leading scientists including Nobel Laureates, then it is safe to explore a cause for this acceleration. Such exploration has led physicists and astronomers to hypothesize a form of energy known as "dark energy," believed to be the force behind the expansion of the universe. Some theories propose that this dark energy accounts for up to 75% of the total energy density in the universe and that it is its anti-gravitational force which accelerates the expansion. Yet dark energy is still theoretical, and it is not known with certainty if it even truly exists, much less how it works, its relationship to spacetime and the expansion of the universe, or if it is a constant or variable form of energy.

As it stands, dark energy is a force shrouded in darkness – a concept that could one day lead to evidence which would help us understand both the origin and the future of the universe.

"Day and night I went without sleep, trying to understand what goes on in this world. I saw everything God does, and I realized that no one can really understand what happens. We may be very wise, but no matter how much we try or how much we claim to know, we cannot understand it all."

Ecclesiastes 8:16-17 CEV

The inner region of Abell 1689, an immense cluster of galaxies located 2.2 billion light-years away. The cluster's gravitational field is warping light from background galaxies, causing them to appear as arcs. The effect is similar to what happens when you look into a fun house mirror. Dark matter in the cluster, which represents about 80 percent of its mass, is mapped by plotting these arcs. Dark matter cannot be photographed, but its distribution is shown in the blue overlay. The dark matter distribution is then used to better understand the nature of dark energy, a pressure that is accelerating the expansion of the universe. NASA/ESA/JPL-CALTECH/YALE/CNRS

Conclusion

"The exquisite order displayed by our scientific understanding of the physical world calls for the divine."

Vera Kistiakowsky,
MIT physicist (1928–)

WE HAVE COME FULL CIRCLE.

We have traveled so far on our round trip starting on Earth and going to the known limits of the universe that we have covered almost 1,000 billion trillion km (620 billion trillion miles), and it has taken us roughly 100 gig light years (2 million billion earth years at the speed of light).

And remember, this is just the part of the universe that is visible to us – the part we can measure and see. What lies beyond nobody knows.

For every new discovery, we uncover an aspect of the divine - of God himself. With such knowledge we also get the precious responsibility to care for all God has given us and to proclaim His greatness with all He has made.

"We are, by astronomical standards, a pampered, cosseted, cherished group of creatures... If the Universe had not been made with the most exacting precision we could never have come into existence. It is my view that these circumstances indicate the universe was created for man to live in."

John O'Keefe,
astronomer at NASA
(1916–2000)

Conclusion

God, the Creator, has made the beauty and mystery and wonder of the universe for His pleasure and glory and for our enjoyment so that we might know Him intimately. He has made it, each part, the beautiful designs and colors of the cosmos, to stir our hearts to seek Him and find Him and know Him.

Is it not a privilege to just watch the work of God? To be a human with such an amazing Creator? The answer to the question "How great is our God?" cannot be explained by words. We need to see it, and what we have seen here is only a small portion of what is out there. But in order to truly grasp God's greatness, we need more than sight. We need something else God has given us – faith.

Is the universe too big for humans? Is it too big compared to its purpose? If the purpose of the universe is to show the greatness of God, and when we consider who He is, it's just about the right size!

"For since the creation of the world God's invisible qualities – his eternal power and divine nature – have been clearly seen, being understood from what has been made, so that people are without excuse.... For the creation waits in eager expectation for the children of God to be revealed. For the creation was subjected to frustration, not by its own choice, but by the will of the one who subjected it, in hope that the creation itself will be liberated from its bondage to decay and brought into the freedom and glory of the children of God." Romans 1:20, 8:19-21NIV

Bibliography

Bahcall, J.N. *Neutrino Astrophysics*. Cambridge: Cambridge University Press, 1989.

Benson, Michael. *Beyond: A Solar System Voyage*. New York: Abrams Books for Young Readers, 2009.

Benson, Michael. *Far out: A Space-time Chronicle*. New York: Abrams, 2009.

Boyle, Alan. *The Case for Pluto: How a Little Planet Made a Big Difference*. Hoboken, N.J.: Wiley & Sons, 2010.

Brown, Mike. *How I Killed Pluto and Why it Had it Coming*. New York: Spiegel & Grau, 2010.

Corfield, R. M. *Lives of the Planets: A Natural History of the Solar System*. New York: Basic Books, 2007.

Conlan Roberta. *Galaxies.* Richmond, Virginia: Time Life Books Inc., 1988

Darling, D. J. *The Universal Book of Astronomy: From the Andromeda Galaxy to the Zone of Avoidance*. Hoboken, NJ: Wiley and Sons, 2003.

DeVorkin, David H., and R. W. Smith. *Hubble: Imaging Space and Time*. Washington, D.C.: National Geographic, 2008.

Glover, L., Patricia Daniels, Jonathan Malay, and Andrea Gianopoulos. National Geographic Encyclopedia of Space. Washington D.C.: National Geographic, 2004: 123.

Gott III, J. R.; Mario Jurić, David Schlegel, Fiona Hoyle, Michael Vogeley, Max Tegmark, Neta Bahcall, Jon Brinkmann. "A Map of the Universe." *The Astrophysics Journal* 624 http://www.astro.princeton.edu/universe/ms.pdf.

John, Duncan. *Astronomy: The Definitive Guide to the Universe*. Bath, UK: Parragon Publishing, 2006.

Jones, T. D., and Ellen R. Stofan. *Planetology: Unlocking the Secrets of the Solar System*. Washington, D.C.: National Geographic, 2008.

Kitchin, Chris. *Galaxies in Turmoil*. Berlin: Springer, 2007.

Lewis, C.S. "God in the Dock: Dogma and the Universe" (Essay). Grand Rapids, Michigan: Wm. B. Eerdmans Publishing Company, 1972.

Mitton, Jacqueline. *Cambridge Illustrated Dictionary of Astronomy*. Cambridge, UK: Cambridge University Press, 2007.

Nielsen, Lotte Juul. *Planeten Jorden*. Bonnier Publications, 2009.

Nielsen, Lotte Juul. *På Rejse i Solsystemet*. Bonnier Publications, 2009.

Nielsen, Lotte Juul. Universets Gåder. Bonnier Publications, 2008.

Rees, Martin. *Universe*. Dorling Kindersley Ltd., 2005.

Redfern, Martin. *The Kingfisher Book of Space*. Kingfisher Publications, 1998

Ridpath, I., and Tirion Will. *Stars and Planets the Most Complete Guide to the Stars, Planets, Galaxies, and the Solar System*. Rev. ed. Princeton, N.J.: Princeton University Press, 2007.

Scagell, R., and David Frydman. *Stargazing with binoculars*. 3rd ed. Ontario, Canada: Firefly Books, 2012.

Sparrow, Giles. *Hubble: Window on the Universe*. New York, NY: Metro Books, 2010.

Spence, Pam. *The Universe Revealed*. Cambridge, U.K.: Cambridge University Press, 1999.

Stott, Carole. *Space: From Earth to the Edge of the Universe*. New York, N.Y.: DK, 2010.

Vanin, Gabriele. *A Photographic Tour of the Universe*. Rev. ed. Ontario, Canada: Firefly Books, 1996.

Winterburn, Emily. *The Stargazer's Guide: How to Read Our Night Sky*. New York, NY: Harper Perennial, 2009.

Bibliography

Ferris, Timothy. "Solar Storms." National Geographic Magazine Online, June 2012, <http://ngm.nationalgeographic.com/2012/06/solar-storms/ferris-text>

Spread 27 http://solarsystem.nasa.gov/planets/index.cfm

Spread 28 http://heasarc.nasa.gov/docs/cosmic/planets.html

Spread 29: How the Sun Works and Life Cycle of a Star diagram <http://www.embracingthenerd.com/wpcontent/uploads/2011/02/the_sun31.jpghttp://nineplanets.org> http://www.loveinfographics.com/wp-content/uploads/2012/01/facts-about-the-sun-science-infographic2.png

Spread 30: http://www.nasa.gov/mission_pages/WISE/multimedia/gallery/neowise/pia15628.html

Spread 43: http://www.universetoday.com/21914/the-closest-galaxy-to-the-milky-way/

Spread 44: http://www.sciencedaily.com/releases/2012/07/120720083011.htm

Spread 45: http://www.dailymail.co.uk/sciencetech/article-2085268/Milky-Way-contain-billions-habitable-planets-reveal-scientists-year-study.html

Spread 46: http://news.nationalgeographic.com/news/2012/03/120323-runaway-planets-hyper-speed-loeb-harvard-space-science/

Spread 47: http://www.space.com/13632-milky-galaxy-midlife-crisis.html

Spread 48: http://news.sciencemag.org/sciencenow/2012/05/the-milky-ways-oldest-and-wisest.html

Spread 49: http://www.universetoday.com/95504/ghostly-jets-haunt-the-milky-ways-black-hole/ http://www.scientificamerican.com/article.cfm?id=milky-way-jets http://www.livescience.com/20622-ghosts-milky-ways-powerful-revealed.html

Lisle, Jason. *Answers in Genesis*. April 15, 2010 <answersingenesis.org>

CERN. The Bulletin. <http://cdsweb.cern.ch/journal/CERNBulletin/2012/37>

New Scientist <http://www.newscientist.com/topic/large-hadron-collider>

Discovery News <http://news.discovery.com>

Universe Today <http://www.universetoday.com>

National Geographic. "Journey to the Edge of the Universe" <http://www.youtube.com/watch?v=wGCOmVQiRNY&feature>

Deep Astronomy <http://www.deepastronomy.com/hypernova-vy-canis-majoris.html>